THE ANCIENT NEAR EASTERN WORLD

== WORLD ==

TEACHING GUIDE

OXFORD

UNIVERSITY PRESS

OXFORD
UNIVERSITY PRESS

Oxford University Press, Inc., publishes works that
further Oxford University's objective of excellence
in research, scholarship, and education.

Oxford   New York
Auckland   Cape Town   Dar es Salaam   Hong Kong   Karachi
Kuala Lumpur   Madrid   Melbourne   Mexico City   Nairobi
New Delhi   Shanghai   Taipei   Toronto

With offices in
Argentina   Austria   Brazil   Chile   Czech Republic   France   Greece
Guatemala   Hungary   Italy   Japan   Poland   Portugal   Singapore
South Korea   Switzerland   Thailand   Turkey   Ukraine   Vietnam

Copyright © 2005 by Oxford University Press, Inc.

Published by Oxford University Press, Inc.
198 Madison Avenue, New York, NY 10016
www.oup.com

Writer: Susan Moger
Editor: Robert Weisser
Project Editor: Lelia Mander
Project Director: Jacqueline A. Ball
Education Consultant: Diane L. Brooks, Ed.D.
Design: designlabnyc

Casper Grathwohl, Publisher

Library of Congress Catalog-in-Publication Data is available
ISBN-13: 978-0-19-522283-8 (California edition)   ISBN-13: 978-0-19-517898-2

Printed in the United States of America
on acid-free paper

CONTENTS

HISTORY FROM OXFORD UNIVERSITY PRESS

"A thoroughly researched political and cultural history... makes for a solid resource for any collection."
– *School Library Journal*

THE WORLD IN ANCIENT TIMES
RONALD MELLOR AND AMANDA H. PODANY, EDS.
THE EARLY HUMAN WORLD
THE ANCIENT NEAR EASTERN WORLD
THE ANCIENT EGYPTIAN WORLD
THE ANCIENT SOUTH ASIAN WORLD
THE ANCIENT CHINESE WORLD
THE ANCIENT GREEK WORLD
THE ANCIENT ROMAN WORLD
THE ANCIENT AMERICAN WORLD

"Bringing history out of the Dark Ages!"

THE MEDIEVAL AND EARLY MODERN WORLD
BONNIE G. SMITH, ED.
THE EUROPEAN WORLD, 400-1450
THE AFRICAN AND MIDDLE EASTERN WORLD, 600-1500
THE ASIAN WORLD, 600-1500
AN AGE OF EMPIRES, 1200-1750
AN AGE OF VOYAGES, 1350-1600
AN AGE OF SCIENCE AND REVOLUTIONS, 1600-1800

"The liveliest, most realistic, most well-received American history series ever written for children."
– *Los Angeles Times*

A HISTORY OF US
JOY HAKIM
THE FIRST AMERICANS
MAKING THIRTEEEN COLONIES
FROM COLONIES TO COUNTRY
THE NEW NATION
LIBERTY FOR ALL?
WAR, TERRIBLE WAR
RECONSTRUCTING AMERICA
AN AGE OF EXTREMES
WAR, PEACE, AND ALL THAT JAZZ
ALL THE PEOPLE

FOR MORE INFORMATION, VISIT US AT WWW.OUP.COM

NOTE TO THE TEACHER

Dear Educator

You probably love history. You read historical novels, watch documentaries, and enjoy (and, as a history teacher, no doubt criticize) Hollywood's attempts to recreate the past. So why don't most kids love history too? We think it might be because of the tone of the history books they are assigned. Many textbook authors seem to assume that the sole goal of teaching history is to make sure the students memorize innumerable facts. So, innumerable facts are crammed onto the pages, facts without context, as thrilling to read as names in a phone book.

Real history, however, is not just facts; it's the story of real people who cared deeply about the events and controversies of their times. And learning real history is essential. It helps children to understand the events that brought the world to where they find it now. It helps them distrust stereotypes of other cultures. It helps them read critically. (It also helps them succeed in standardized assessments of their reading skills.) We, like you, find history positively addictive. Students can feel the same way. (Can you imagine a child reading a history book with a flashlight after lights out, just because it is so interesting?)

The World in Ancient Times books reveal ancient history to be a great story—a whole bunch of great stories—some of which have been known for centuries, but some of which are just being discovered. Each book in the series is written by a team of two writers: a scholar who is working in the field of ancient history and knows what is new and exciting, and a well-known children's book author who knows how to communicate these ideas to kids. The teams have come up with books that are historically accurate and up to date as well as beautifully written. They also feature magnificent illustrations of real artifacts, archaeological sites, and works of art, along with maps and timelines to allow readers to get a sense of where events are set in place and time. Etymologies from the *Oxford English Dictionary*, noted in the margins, help to expand students' vocabulary by identifying the ancient roots, along with the meanings, of English words.

The authors of our books use vivid language to describe what we know and to present the evidence for *how* we know what we know. We let the readers puzzle right along with the historians and archaeologists. The evidence comes in the form of primary sources, not only in the illustrations but especially in the documents written in ancient times, which are quoted extensively.

You can integrate these primary sources into lessons with your students. When they read a document or look at an artifact or building in the illustrations they can pose questions and make hypotheses about the culture it came from. Why was a king shown as much larger than his attendants in an Egyptian relief sculpture? Why was Pliny unsure about what to do with accused Christians in his letter to the emperor? In this way, students can think like historians.

The series provides a complete narrative for a yearlong course on ancient history. You might choose to have your students read all eight narrative books as they learn about each of the civilizations in turn (or fewer than eight, depending on the ancient civilizations covered in your school's curriculum). Or you might choose to highlight certain chapters in each of the books, and use the others for extended activities or research projects. Since each chapter is written to stand on its own, the students will not be confused if you don't assign all of them. The *Primary Sources and Reference Volume* provides longer primary sources than are available in the other books, allowing students to make their own interpretations and comparisons across cultures.

The ancient world was the stage on which many institutions that we think of as modern were first played out: law, cities, legitimate government, technology, and so on. The major world religions all had their origins long ago, before 600 CE, as did many of the great cities of the world. *The World in Ancient Times* presents this ancient past in a new way—new not just to young adults, but to any audience. The scholarship is top-notch and the telling will catch you up in the thrill of exploration and discovery.

Amanda H. Podany and Ronald Mellor
General Editors, *The World in Ancient Times*

I. STUDENT EDITION

▶ Engaging, friendly narrative
▶ A wide range of primary sources in every chapter
▶ The authority of Oxford scholarship
▶ Period illustrations and specially commissioned maps

Ronald Mellor
& Marni McGee

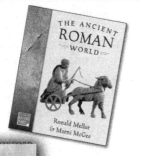

II. TEACHING GUIDE

▶ Wide range of activities and classroom approaches
▶ Strategies for universal access and improving literacy (ELL, struggling readers, advanced learners)
▶ Multiple assessment tools

III. STUDENT STUDY GUIDE

▶ Exercises correlated to Student Edition and Teaching Guide
▶ Portfolio approach
▶ Activities for every level of learning
▶ Literacy through reading and writing

PRIMARY SOURCES AND REFERENCE VOLUME

▶ Broad selection of primary sources in each subject area
▶ Ideal resource for in-class exercises and unit projects

TEACHING GUIDE: KEY FEATURES

The Teaching Guides organize each *The World in Ancient Times* book into units, usually of three or four chapters each. The chapters in each unit cover a key span of time or have a common theme, such as a civilization's origins, government, religion, economy, and daily life.

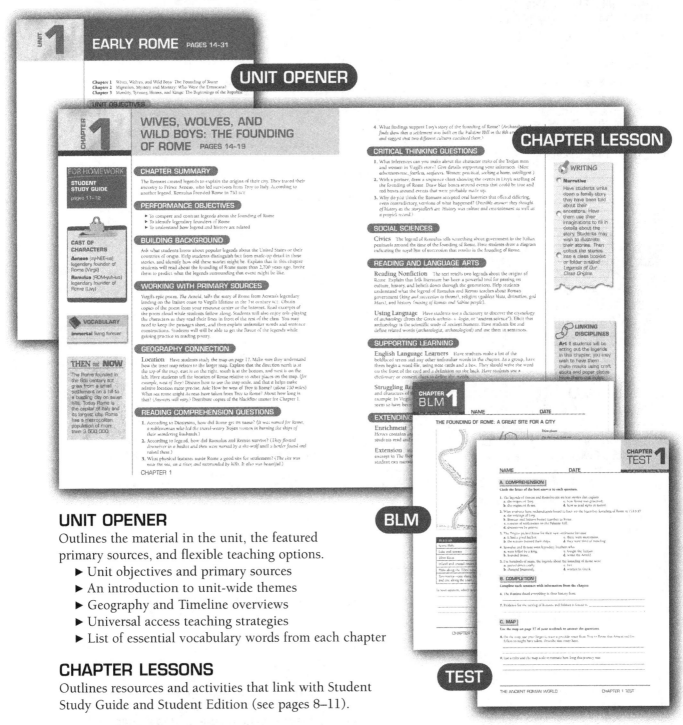

UNIT OPENER
Outlines the material in the unit, the featured primary sources, and flexible teaching options.
  ▶ Unit objectives and primary sources
  ▶ An introduction to unit-wide themes
  ▶ Geography and Timeline overviews
  ▶ Universal access teaching strategies
  ▶ List of essential vocabulary words from each chapter

CHAPTER LESSONS
Outlines resources and activities that link with Student Study Guide and Student Edition (see pages 8–11).

TESTS AND BLACKLINE MASTERS (BLMS)
Reproducible tests and exercises for assessment, homework, or classroom projects

Organized so that you can easily find the information you need.

CHAPTER SUMMARY AND PERFORMANCE OBJECTIVES

The Chapter Summary gives an overview of the information in the chapter. The Performance Objectives are the three or four important goals students should achieve in the chapter. Accomplishing these goals will help students master the information in the book.

BUILDING BACKGROUND

This section connects students to the chapter they are about to read. Students may be asked to use what they know to make predictions about the text, preview the images in the chapter, or connect modern life with the ancient subject matter.

WORKING WITH PRIMARY SOURCES

A major feature of *The World in Ancient Times* is having students read about history through the words and images of the people who lived it. Each book includes excerpts from the best sources from these ancient civilizations, giving the narrative an immediacy that is difficult to match in secondary sources. Students can read further in these sources on their own or in small groups using the accompanying *The World in Ancient Times Primary Sources and Reference Volume*. The Teaching Guide recommends activities so students of all skill levels can appreciate the ways people from the past saw themselves, their ideas and values, and their fears and dreams.

CHAPTER 1

WIVES, WOLVES, AND WILD BOYS: THE FOUNDING OF ROME PAGES 14–19

FOR HOMEWORK

STUDENT STUDY GUIDE
pages 11–12

CAST OF CHARACTERS

Aeneas (ay-NEE-us) legendary founder of Rome (Virgil)

Romulus (ROM-yuh-lus) legendary founder of Rome (Livy)

VOCABULARY

immortal living forever

THEN and **NOW**
The Rome founded in the 8th century BCE grew from a small settlement on a hill to a bustling city on seven hills. Today Rome is the capital of Italy and its largest city. Rome has a metropolitan population of more than 3,500,000.

CHAPTER SUMMARY

The Romans created legends to explain the origins of their city. They traced their ancestry to Prince Aeneas, who led survivors from Troy to Italy. According to another legend, Romulus founded Rome in 753 BCE.

PERFORMANCE OBJECTIVES

▸ To compare and contrast legends about the founding of Rome
▸ To identify legendary founders of Rome
▸ To understand how legend and history are related

BUILDING BACKGROUND

Ask what students know about popular legends about the United States or their countries of origin. Help students distinguish fact from made-up detail in these stories, and identify how old these stories might be. Explain that in this chapter students will read about the founding of Rome more than 2,700 years ago. Invite them to predict what the legends surrounding that event might be like.

WORKING WITH PRIMARY SOURCES

Virgil's epic poem, *The Aeneid*, tells the story of Rome from Aeneas's legendary landing on the Italian coast to Virgil's lifetime in the 1st century BCE. Obtain copies of the poem from your resource center or the Internet. Read excerpts of the poem aloud while students follow along. Students will also enjoy role-playing the characters as they read their lines in front of the rest of the class. You may need to keep the passages short, and then explain unfamiliar words and sentence constructions. Students will still be able to get the flavor of the legends while gaining practice in reading poetry.

GEOGRAPHY CONNECTION

Location Have students study the map on page 17. Make sure they understand how the inset map relates to the larger map. Explain that the direction north is at the top of the map, east is on the right, south is at the bottom, and west is on the left. Have students tell the location of Rome relative to other places on the map. (*for example, west of Troy*) Discuss how to use the map scale, and that it helps make relative location more precise. Ask: How far west of Troy is Rome? (*about 750 miles*) What sea route might Aeneas have taken from Troy to Rome? About how long is that? (*Answers will vary.*) Distribute copies of the blackline master for Chapter 1.

READING COMPREHENSION QUESTIONS

1. According to Dionysius, how did Rome get its name? (*It was named for Roma, a noblewoman who led the travel-weary Trojan women in burning the ships of their wandering husbands.*)
2. According to legend, how did Romulus and Remus survive? (*They floated downriver in a basket and then were nursed by a she-wolf until a herder found and raised them.*)
3. What physical features made Rome a good site for settlement? (*The site was near the sea, on a river, and surrounded by hills. It also was beautiful.*)

CHAPTER 1

GEOGRAPHY CONNECTION

Each chapter has a Geography Connection to strengthen students' map skills as well as their understanding of how geography affects human civilization. One of the five themes of geography (Location, Interaction, Movement, Place, and Regions) is highlighted in each chapter. Map skills such as reading physical, political, and historical maps; using latitude and longitude to find locations; and using the features of a map (mileage scale, legend) are taught throughout the book and reinforced in blackline masters.

4. What findings support Livy's story of the founding of Rome? (*Archaeological finds show that a settlement was built on the Palatine Hill in the 8th century BCE and suggest that two different cultures coexisted there.*)

CRITICAL THINKING QUESTIONS

1. What inferences can you make about the character traits of the Trojan men and women in Virgil's story? Give details supporting your inferences. (*Men: adventuresome, fearless, seafarers. Women: practical, seeking a home, intelligent.*)

2. With a partner, draw a sequence chart showing the events in Livy's retelling of the founding of Rome. Draw blue boxes around events that could be true and red boxes around events that were probably made up.

3. Why do you think the Romans accepted oral histories that offered differing, even contradictory, versions of what happened? (*Possible answer: they thought of history as the storyteller's art. History was culture and entertainment as well as a people's record.*)

SOCIAL SCIENCES

Civics The legend of Romulus tells something about government in the Italian peninsula around the time of the founding of Rome. Have students draw a diagram indicating the royal line of succession that results in the founding of Rome.

READING AND LANGUAGE ARTS

Reading Nonfiction The text retells two legends about the origins of Rome. Explain that folk literature has been a powerful tool for passing on culture, history, and beliefs down through the generations. Help students understand what the legend of Romulus and Remus teaches about Roman government (*king and succession to throne*), religion (*goddess Vesta, divination, god Mars*), and history (*mixing of Roman and Sabine people*).

Using Language Have students use a dictionary to discover the etymology of *archaeology* (from the Greek *archaio-* + *-logia*, or "ancient science"). Elicit that archaeology is the scientific study of ancient humans. Have students list and define related words (*archaeologist, archaeological*) and use them in sentences.

SUPPORTING LEARNING

English Language Learners Have students make a list of the boldfaced terms and any other unfamiliar words in the chapter. As a group, have them begin a word file, using note cards and a box. They should write the word on the front of the card and a definition on the back. Have students use a dictionary or context clues to define the words.

Struggling Readers Have students make a chart comparing the events and characters of the two legends. Then help students draw conclusions: for example, in Virgil, the founders of Rome came from Troy; in Livy, the founders seem to have been living in Italy already.

EXTENDING LEARNING

Enrichment Edith Hamilton's book *Mythology: Timeless Tales of Gods and Heroes* contains another myth about the founding of Rome by Aeneas. Have students read and summarize this myth for the class.

Extension Have student groups act out scenes from *The Aeneid*, from the excerpt in *The World in Ancient Times Primary Sources and Reference Volume*. One student can narrate while the others take the parts of the characters involved.

THE ANCIENT ROMAN WORLD

 WRITING

Narrative
Have students write down a family story they have been told about their ancestors. Have them use their imaginations to fill in details about the story. Students may wish to illustrate their stories. Then collect the stories into a class booklet or folder entitled *Legends of Our Class Origins.*

LINKING DISCIPLINES

Art If students will be acting out the legends in this chapter, you may wish to have them make masks using craft sticks and paper plates. Have them cut holes for eyes and mouth. They can model their characters' features after the pictures of Roman men and women in Chapters 1–3.

READING COMPREHENSION AND CRITICAL THINKING QUESTIONS

The reading comprehension questions are general enough to allow free-flowing class or small group discussion, yet specific enough to be used for oral or written assessment of students' grasp of the important information. The critical thinking questions are intended to engage students in a deeper analysis of the text and can also be used for oral or written assessment.

SOCIAL SCIENCES ACTIVITIES

Students can use these activities to connect the subject matter in the Student Edition with other areas in the social sciences: economics, civics, and science, technology, and society.

READING AND LANGUAGE ARTS

These activities serve a twofold purpose: Some are designed to facilitate the development of nonfiction reading strategies. Others can be used to help students' appreciation of fiction and poetry, as well as nonfiction, by dealing with concepts such as word choice, description, and figurative language.

SUPPORTING LEARNING AND EXTENDING LEARNING

Each chapter gives suggestions for students of varying abilities and learning styles; for example, advanced learners, below-level readers, auditory/visual/tactile learners, and English language learners. These may be individual, partner, or group activities, and may or may not require your ongoing supervision.
(For more on Supporting or Extending Learning sections, see pages 16–19.)

Icons quickly help to identify key concepts, facts, activities, and assessment activities in the sidebars.

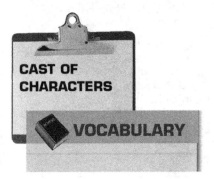

▶ Cast of Characters/Vocabulary

These sidebars point out and identify bolded, curriculum-specific vocabulary words and significant personalities in the chapter. Pronunciation guides are included where necessary. Additional important vocabulary words are listed in each unit opener.

▶ Writing

Each chapter has a suggestion for a specific writing assignment. You can make these assignments as you see fit—to help students meet state requirements in writing as well as to help individual students improve their skills. Areas of writing covered include the following:

Description	Personal writing (journal/diary)
Narration	News article (print and electronic)
Explanation	Dialogue
Persuasion	Interview
Composition	Poetry

▶ Then and Now

This feature provides interesting facts and ideas about the ancient civilization and relates it to the modern world. This may be an aspect of government that we still use today, word origins of common modern expressions, physical reminders of the past that are still evident, and other features. You can use this item simply to promote interest in the subject matter or as a springboard to other research.

▶ Linking Disciplines

This feature offers opportunities to investigate other subject areas that relate to the material in the Student Edition: math, science, arts, and health. Specific areas of these subjects are emphasized: **Math** (arithmetic, algebra, geometry, data, statistics); **Science** (life science, earth science, physical science); **Arts** (music, arts, dance, drama, architecture); **Health** (personal health, world health).

▶ For Homework

A quick glance links you to additional activities in the Student Study Guide that can be assigned as homework.

ASSESSMENT

The World in Ancient Times program intentionally omits from the Student Edition the kinds of section, chapter, and unit questions that are used to review and assess learning in standard textbooks. It is the purpose of the series to engage readers in learning—and loving—history written as good literature. Rather than interrupting student reading, and enjoyment, all assessment instruments for the series have been placed in the Teaching Guides.

▶ CHAPTER TESTS

A reproducible chapter test follows each chapter in this Teaching Guide. These tests will help you assess students' mastery of the content standards addressed in each chapter. These tests measure a variety of cognitive and analytical skills, particularly comprehension, critical thinking, and expository writing, through multiple choice, short answer, and essay questions.
An answer key for the chapter tests is provided at the end of the Teaching Guide.

▶ WRAP-UP TEST

After the last chapter test you will find a wrap-up test consisting of 10 essay questions that evaluate students' ability to synthesize and express what they've learned about the ancient civilization under study.

▶ RUBRICS

The rubrics at the back of this Teaching Guide will help you assess students' written work, oral presentations, and group projects. They include a Scoring Rubric, based on the California State Public School standards for good writing and effective cooperative learning. In addition, a simplified hand-out is provided, plus a form for evaluating group projects and a Library/Media Center Research Log to help students focus and evaluate their research. Students can also evaluate their own work using these rubrics.

▶ BLACKLINE MASTERS (BLMs)

A blackline master follows each chapter in the Teaching Guide. These BLMs are reproducible pages for you to use as in-class activities or homework exercises. They can also be used for assessment as needed.

▶ ADDITIONAL ASSESSMENT ACTIVITIES

Each unit opener includes suggestions for using one or more unit projects for assessment. These points, and the rubrics provided, will help you evaluate how your students are progressing towards meeting the unit objectives.

USING THE STUDENT STUDY GUIDE FOR ASSESSMENT

▶ Study Guide Activities
Assignments in the Student Study Guide correspond with those in the Teaching Guide. If needed, these Student Study Guide activities can be used for assessment.

▶ Portfolio Approach
Student Study Guide pages can be removed from the workbook and turned in for grading. When the pages are returned, they can be part of the students' individual history journals. Have students keep a 3-ring binder portfolio of Study Guide pages, alongside writing projects and other activities.

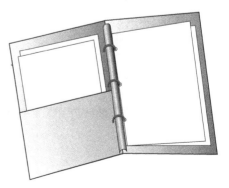

The Student Study Guide works as both standalone instructional material and as a support to the Student Edition and this Teaching Guide. Certain activities encourage informal small-group or family participation. These features make it an effective teaching tool:

Flexibility

You can use the Study Guide in the classroom, with individuals or small groups, or send it home for homework. You can distribute the entire guide to students; however, the pages are perforated so you can remove and distribute only the pertinent lessons.

A page on reports and special projects in the front of the Study Guide directs students to the Further Reading resource in the student edition. This feature gives students general guidance on doing research and devising independent study projects of their own.

FACSIMILE SPREAD

The Study Guide begins with a facsimile spread from the Student Edition. This spread gives reading strategies and highlights key features: captions, primary sources, sidebars, headings, etymologies. The spread supplies the contextualization students need to fully understand the material.

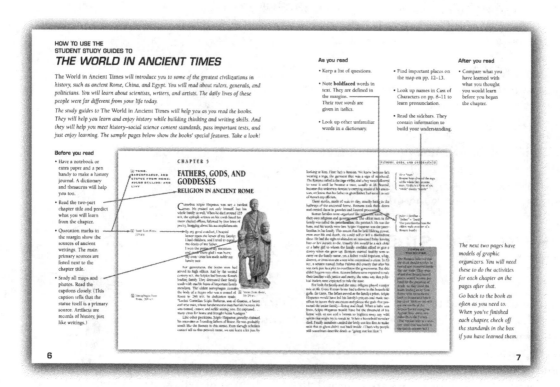

Portfolio Approach

The Study Guide pages are three-hole-punched so they can be integrated with notebook paper in a looseleaf binder. This history journal or portfolio can become both a record of content mastery and an outlet for each student's unique creative expression. Responding to prompts, students can write poetry or songs, plays and character sketches, create storyboards or cartoons, or construct multi-layered timelines.

The portfolio approach gives students unlimited opportunities for practice in areas that need strengthening. Students cam share their journals and compare their work. And the Study Guide pages in the portfolio make a valuable assessment tool for you. It is an ongoing record of performance that can be reviewed and graded periodically.

GRAPHIC ORGANIZERS

This feature contains reduced models of seven graphic organizers referenced frequently in the guide. Using these devices will help students organize the material so it is meaningful to them. (Full-size reproducibles of each graphic organizer are provided at the back of this Teaching Guide.) These graphic organizers include: outline, main idea map, K-W-L chart (What I Know, What I Want to Know, What I Learned), Venn diagram, timeline, sequence of events chart, and T-chart.

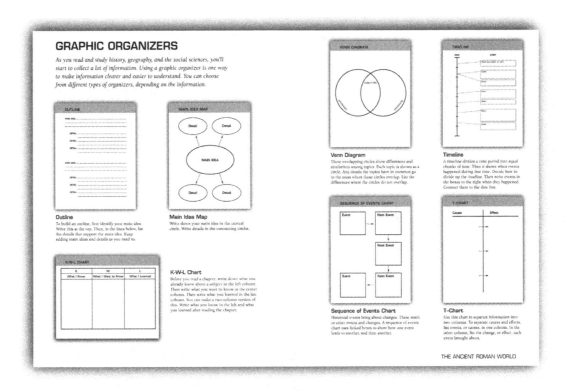

Each chapter lesson is designed to draw students into the subject matter. Recurring features and exercises challenge their knowledge and allow them to practice valuable analysis skills. Activities in the Teaching Guide and Student Study Guide complement but do not duplicate each other. Together they offer a wide range of class work, group projects, and opportunities for further study and assessment that can be tailored to all ability levels.

CHAPTER SUMMARY
briefly reviews big ideas from the chapter.

ACCESS
invites students into the content by building background, tapping prior knowledge, or visual note-taking.

ADDITIONAL VOCABULARY
Additional vocabulary words important to accessing student book content are listed on page 10 of every Student Study Guide.

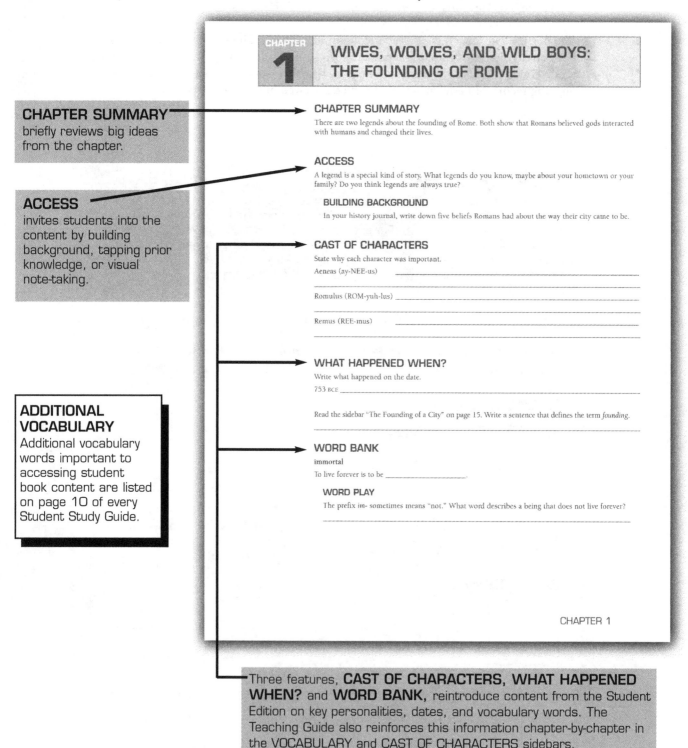

CHAPTER 1

WIVES, WOLVES, AND WILD BOYS: THE FOUNDING OF ROME

CHAPTER SUMMARY
There are two legends about the founding of Rome. Both show that Romans believed gods interacted with humans and changed their lives.

ACCESS
A legend is a special kind of story. What legends do you know, maybe about your hometown or your family? Do you think legends are always true?

BUILDING BACKGROUND
In your history journal, write down five beliefs Romans had about the way their city came to be.

CAST OF CHARACTERS
State why each character was important.
Aeneas (ay-NEE-us) _____

Romulus (ROM-yuh-lus) _____

Remus (REE-mus) _____

WHAT HAPPENED WHEN?
Write what happened on the date.
753 BCE _____

Read the sidebar "The Founding of a City" on page 15. Write a sentence that defines the term *founding*.
_____

WORD BANK
immortal
To live forever is to be _____.

WORD PLAY
The prefix *im-* sometimes means "not." What word describes a being that does not live forever?
_____

CHAPTER 1

Three features, **CAST OF CHARACTERS, WHAT HAPPENED WHEN?** and **WORD BANK**, reintroduce content from the Student Edition on key personalities, dates, and vocabulary words. The Teaching Guide also reinforces this information chapter-by-chapter in the VOCABULARY and CAST OF CHARACTERS sidebars.

CRITICAL THINKING
CAUSE AND EFFECT

Draw a line from each cause and connect it to the result, or effect. (There is one extra effect.)

CAUSE	EFFECT
1. Amulius feared he would be overthrown,	a. they floated down the river and were saved by a she-wolf.
2. Rhea Silvia broke her vows,	
3. A servant couldn't kill the babies,	b. the Romans and Sabines went to war.
4. Remus made fun of Romulus,	c. Romulus killed Remus.
5. Romulus's men kidnapped Sabine women,	d. Romans and Sabines called a truce
6. The Sabine women ran onto the battlefield,	e. Romulus and Remus were born.
	f. he forced Rhea Silvia to join the Vestal Virgins.
	g. Remus killed Romulus.

WITH A PARENT OR PARTNER

When you have completed the chart, read aloud each cause-and-effect pairing to a parent or partner. Use the word "so" to connect each cause with each effect.

WRITE ABOUT IT

The Trojan women were *appalled* that Aeneas and the Trojan men were planning another journey after they reached the mouth of the Tiber River. To be *appalled* means to be

a) happy.

b) excited.

c) shocked.

Circle your answer.

In your history journal, write a short dialogue or a descriptive scene between the Trojan men and women about making this second journey. Why were the women appalled? How did the men respond?

WORKING WITH PRIMARY SOURCES

The image at left is an ancient Roman coin. It shows an image of a Roman god. Think about what we can learn about ancient cultures through artifacts like this one. Answer the following questions in your history journal.

1. Why do you think the figure is wearing an olive wreath?

2. Why would the Romans put a god on their coins?

3. What famous people do we use on coins today? (It's okay to take a peek at your pocket change!)

4. If people found your coins hundreds of years from now, what conclusions might they draw about your culture?

5. Think up a design for your own coin and draw it in your history journal.

THE ANCIENT ROMAN WORLD

CRITICAL THINKING exercises draw on such thinking skills as establishing cause and effect, making inferences, drawing conclusions, determining sequence of events, comparing and contrasting, identifying main ideas and details, and other analytical process.

WRITE ABOUT IT gives students writing suggestions drawn from the material. A writing assignment may stem from a vocabulary word, a historical event, or a reading of a primary source. The assignment can take any number of forms: newspaper article, letter, short essay, a scene with dialogue, a diary entry.

WORKING WITH PRIMARY SOURCES invites students to read primary sources closely. Exercises include answering comprehension questions, evaluating point of view, and writing and other forms of creative expression, including music, art, and design. "In Your Own Words" writing activities ask students to paraphrase a primary source.

IMPROVING LITERACY WITH THE WORLD IN ANCIENT TIMES

The books in this series are written in a lively, narrative style to inspire a love of reading history–social science. English language learners and struggling readers are given special consideration within the program's exercises and activities. And students who love to read and learn will also benefit from the program's rich and varied material. Following are strategies to make sure each and every student gets the most out of the subjects you will teach through *The World in Ancient Times*.

ENGLISH LANGUAGE LEARNERS

For English learners to achieve academic success, the instructional considerations for teachers include two mandates:

- Help them attain grade level, content area knowledge, and academic language.
- Provide for the development of English language proficiency.

To accomplish these goals, you should plan lessons that reflect the student's level of English proficiency. Students progress through five developmental levels as they increase in language proficiency:

Beginning and Early Intermediate *(grade level material will be mostly incomprehensible, students need a great deal of teacher support)*

Intermediate *(grade level work will be a challenge)*

Early Advanced and Advanced *(close to grade level reading and writing, students continue to need support)*

The books in this program are written at the intermediate level. However, you can still use the lesson plans for students of different levels by using the strategies below:

Tap Prior Knowledge
What students know about the topic will help determine your next steps for instruction. Using K-W-L charts, brainstorming, and making lists are ways to find out what they know. English learners bring a rich cultural diversity into the classroom. By sharing what they know, students can connect their knowledge and experiences to the course.

Set the Context
Use different tools to make new information understandable. These can be images, artifacts, maps, timelines, illustrations, charts, videos, or graphic organizers. Techniques such as role-playing and story-boarding can also be helpful. Speak in shorter sentences, with careful enunciation, expanded explanations, repetitions, and paraphrasing. Use fewer idiomatic expressions.

Show—Don't Just Tell
English learners often get lost as they listen to directions, explanations, lectures, and discussions. By showing students what is expected, you can help them participate more fully in classroom activities. Students need to be shown how to use the graphic organizers in this guide and the mini versions in the student study guide, as well as other blackline masters for note-taking and practice. An overhead transparency with whole or small groups is also effective.

Use the Text

Because of unfamiliar words, students will need help. Teach them to preview the chapter using text features (headings, bold print, sidebars, italics). See the suggestions in the facsimile of the Student Edition, shown on pages 6–7 of the Student Study Guide. Show students organizing structures such as cause and effect or comparing and contrasting. Have students read to each other in pairs. Encourage them to share their history journals with each other. Use Read Aloud/Think Aloud, perhaps with an overhead transparency. Help them create word banks, charts, and graphic organizers. Discuss the main idea after reading.

Check for Understanding

Rather than simply ask students if they understand, stop frequently and ask them to paraphrase or expand on what you just said. Such techniques will give you a much clearer assessment of their understanding.

Provide for Interaction

As students interact with the information and speak their thoughts, their content knowledge and academic language skills improve. Increase interaction in the classroom through cooperative learning, small group work, and partner share. By working and talking with others, students can practice asking and answering questions.

Use Appropriate Assessment

When modifying the instruction, you will also need to modify the assessment. Multiple choice, true and false, and other criterion reference tests are suitable, but consider changing test format and structure. English learners are constantly improving their language proficiency in their oral and written responses, but they are often grammatically incorrect. Remember to be thoughtful and fair about giving students credit for their content knowledge and use of academic language, even if their English isn't perfect.

STRUGGLING READERS

Some students struggle to understand the information presented in a textbook. The following strategies for content-area reading can help students improve their ability to make comparisons, sequence events, determine importance, summarize, evaluate, synthesize, analyze, and solve problems.

Build Knowledge of Genre

Both the fiction and narrative nonfiction genres are incorporated into *The World in Ancient Times*. This combination of genres makes the text interesting and engaging. But teachers must be sure students can identify and use the organizational structures of both genres.

Fiction	Nonfiction
Each chapter is a story	Content: historical information
Setting: historical time and place	Organizational structure: cause/effect, sequence of events, problem/solution
Characters: historical figures	Other features: maps, timelines, sidebars, photographs, primary sources
Plot: problems, roadblocks, and resolutions	

In addition, the textbook has a wealth of the text features of nonfiction: bold and italic print, sidebars, headings and subheadings, labels, captions, and "signal words" such as *first*, *next*, and *finally*. Teaching these organizational structures and text features is essential for struggling readers.

Build Background

Having background information about a topic makes reading about it so much easier. When students lack background information, teachers can preteach or "front load" concepts and vocabulary, using a variety of instructional techniques. Conduct a chapter or book walk, looking at titles, headings, and other text features to develop a big picture of the content. Focus on new vocabulary words during the "walk" and create a word bank with illustrations for future reference. Read aloud key passages and discuss the meaning. Focus on the timeline and maps to help students develop a sense of time and place. Show a video, go to a website, and have trade books and magazines on the topic available for student exploration.

Comprehension Strategies

While reading, successful readers are predicting, making connections, monitoring, visualizing, questioning, inferring, and summarizing. Struggling readers have a harder time with these "in the head" processes. The following strategies will help these students construct meaning from the text until they are able to do it on their own.

> **PREDICT:** Before reading, conduct a picture and text feature "tour" of the chapter to make predictions. Ask students if they remember if this has ever happened before, to predict what might happen this time.

> **MAKE CONNECTIONS:** Help students relate content to their background (text to text, text to self, and text to the world).

> **MONITOR AND CONFIRM:** Encourage students to stop reading when they come across an unknown word, phrase, or concept. In their notebooks, have them make a note of text they don't understand and ask for clarification or figure it out. While this activity slows down reading at first, it is effective in improving skills over time.

> **VISUALIZE:** Students benefit from imagining the events described in a story. Sketching scenes, story-boarding, role-playing, and looking for sensory details all help students with this strategy.

> **INFER:** Help students look beyond the literal meaning of a text to understand deeper meanings. Graphic organizers and discussions provide opportunities to broaden their understanding. Looking closely at the "why" of historical events helps students infer.

> **QUESTION AND DISCUSS:** Have students jot down their questions as they read, and then share them during discussions. Or have students come up with the type of questions they think a teacher would ask. Over time students will develop more complex inferential questions, which lead to group discussions. Questioning and discussing also helps students see ideas from multiple perspectives and draw conclusions, both critical skills for understanding history.

DETERMINE IMPORTANCE: Teach students how to decide what is most important from all the facts and details in nonfiction. After reading for an overall understanding, they can go back to highlight important ideas, words, and phrases. Clues for determining importance include bold or italic print, signal words, and other text features. A graphic organizer such as a main idea map also helps.

Teach and Practice Decoding Strategies

Rather than simply defining an unfamiliar word, teach struggling readers decoding strategies:

- Have them look at the prefix, suffix, and root to help figure out the new word.

- Look for words they know within the word.

- Use the context for clues, and read further or reread.

ADVANCED LEARNERS

Every classroom has students who finish the required assignments and then want additional challenges. Fortunately, the very nature of history and social science offers a wide range of opportunities for students to explore topics in greater depth. Encourage them to come up with their own ideas for an additional assignment. Determine the final product, its presentation, and a timeline for completion.

▶ Research

Students can develop in-depth understanding through seeking information, exploring ideas, asking and answering questions, making judgments, considering points of view, and evaluating actions and events. They will need access to a wide range of resource materials: the Internet, maps, encyclopedias, trade books, magazines, dictionaries, artifacts, newspapers, museum catalogues, brochures, and the library. See the Further Reading section at the end of the Student Edition for good jumping-off points.

▶ Projects

You can encourage students to capitalize on their strengths as learners (visual, verbal, kinesthetic, or musical) or to try a new way of responding. Students can prepare a debate or write a persuasive paper, play, skit, poem, song, dance, game, puzzle, or biography. They can create an alphabet book on the topic, film a video, do a book talk, or illustrate a book. They can render charts, graphs, or other visual representations. Allow for creativity and support students' thinking.

Cheryl A. Caldera, M.A.
Literacy Coach

UNIT 1

ORIGINS OF CIVILIZATION

PAGES 16–42

Chapter 1   Ancient Trash and Buried Treasure: Archaeologists at Work
Chapter 2   Rivers and Ditches, Temples and Farms: Irrigation and the Growth of Towns
Chapter 3   Of Potters and Pots, Plowmen and Plows: Technology and the First Cities
Chapter 4   How Words Changed the World: The Invention of Writing

UNIT OBJECTIVES

Unit 1 covers the period from the dawn of writing in Mesopotamia more than 10,000 years ago through the early settlements in the Fertile Crescent and the innovations that made Mesopotamian civilization flourish almost 7,000 years later. In this unit, your students will learn

▶ how archaeologists learn about ancient civilizations.
▶ how irrigation and religious beliefs helped the growth of towns.
▶ how early developments in technology spawned trade, long-distance communication, and civilization.
▶ how the development of writing revolutionized the way of life in the Near East.

PRIMARY SOURCES

Unit 1 includes excerpts from the following primary sources:

▶ "The Lamentation over the Destruction of Sumer and Akkad," Iraq, about 2000 BCE
▶ List, Iraq, 18th century BCE
▶ Messenger tablet, Iraq 2040 BCE
▶ Personal letter, Iraq, 18th or 17th century BCE

Pictures of artifacts from the earliest Mesopotamian times can also be analyzed as primary sources:

▶ Tell (hill) at Jericho
▶ Gold headband from Umm el-Marra, Syria, 2300 BCE
▶ Tomb at Umm el-Marra, Syria
▶ Donkey skulls, Umm el-Marra, Syria
▶ Alabaster carving, Iraq
▶ Pots, Iraq, 3500 BCE
▶ Clay potter's wheel
▶ Cylinder seal impression of a plow, Mesopotamia
▶ Mosaic of chariot
▶ Wall mosaic, temple at Uruk
▶ Mesopotamian clay tokens
▶ Tablet of pictographic script
▶ Mesopotamian cuneiform

BIG IDEAS IN UNIT 1

Technology and **innovation** are the big ideas presented in Unit 1. The unit discusses the technology developed by the ancient Near Eastern peoples to wrest a living from their hot, dry land; and the innovation of writing that expanded communication and trade and allows us to learn more about these peoples.

Ask students to describe cutting-edge technology today, and elicit fields in which innovation is in the news. Relate the excitement and wonder at the newest advance in computers or electronics or automotives to the excitement of having more efficient ways of getting water to crops (irrigation) or getting products to market (wheeled carts and wagons).

GEOGRAPHY CONNECTION

The Introduction deals with an important concept for understanding the ancient Near East: as opposed to other periods of world history, boundaries between ancient lands are not easy to ascertain, and so the region is often studied as an entirety. Have students compare the map on pages 12–13 to a modern map of the Middle East to get a better idea of the countries that make up this region.

TIMELINE

8000 BCE	Tokens used for accounts
5000 BCE	First towns in southern Mesopotamia settled
3800 BCE	"Uruk period" begins
3800–3100 BCE	Plow invented
3500 BCE	First cities in Mesopotamia
3500 BCE	Potter's wheel invented
3200 BCE	Picture-based writing invented
3100 BCE	Wheel and wagon invented
3100 BCE	Mesopotamians establish first colonies
3000s BCE	Mesopotamians producing cloth from wool
3000 BCE	First cuneiform writing
2600 BCE	First known royal inscription
2400 BCE	First personal letters

UNIT PROJECTS

Drama

Groups of students can create skits based on the material in these chapters. For example, students can show the development of writing from the earliest record-keeping tokens through tokens sent as messages and tokens sent in sealed clay envelopes and so on in a series of skits involving one person trying to communicate with another. Students should make up props necessary for their skits.

Chronology

Students can create a class timeline to show the sequence of events in this unit. The concentration should not necessarily be on dates, but rather on the cause-and-effect chain of events that makes up history. You may want to draw the timeline itself on poster board, and have students write specific dates and events on note cards and attach them in the appropriate places. (Most of the dates, up until about 1000 BCE, will be approximate). Students can then copy the timelines into their notebooks for later review and extension in other units.

Early Town Plans

Small groups can use the information in Chapter 2, including the diagram of fields by the river on page 27, to make their own diagrams of how the villages of southern Mesopotamia developed. Students' diagrams should indicate the sites of shrines in the village, sections of houses, irrigation canals, and the river. Students can use different symbols for different features of their diagrams, and create a key explaining them. Have students display their work in the classroom.

Research Report

Small groups of students can investigate subjects of their choice to bring more information back to the rest of the class. Possible subjects include cuneiform writing, ancient irrigation techniques, and advances in technology such as the potter's wheel, cart, and wagon. Students can use the sources found in Further Reading and Websites at the back of their books. Groups can create a panel discussion or a visual display to explain the information to the class.

ADDITIONAL ASSESSMENT

For Unit 1, divide the class into groups and have them all undertake the Research Report project so you can assess their understanding of the innovations that made civilization in Mesopotamia possible. Use the scoring rubric at the back of this guide to assess students' work, and have students rate their own work with the self-assessment rubric.

UNIVERSAL ACCESS

The exciting narrative of *The Ancient Near Eastern World* will hold students' interest and encourage all students to enjoy learning about the ancient Near East. The following strategies are designed to cover a range of learning styles and reading, language, and skill levels. This section includes suggestions to help differentiate instruction to meet the needs of a diverse student population, and you may find that any of your students will benefit from various strategies presented. Select the most appropriate activities for the needs of the students in your class.

Reading Strategies

▶ To facilitate reading, point out text features such as side-column notes, captions, definitions, and other graphic aids that students will encounter as they read. Help students understand that these features relate to the main text and help them more fully understand the material. As you read chapters with students, call on volunteers to read these special features.

▶ There will be many unfamiliar names of people and places in these chapters. Make students aware of the Cast of Characters in the front of their book. If a name doesn't appear there, you may be able to find it in an encyclopedia or biographical dictionary. Say each name several times and then write it on the board. Help students associate the spoken word with the written word.

▶ Have partners read the text together. Suggest that one student read a section aloud, and then the other paraphrase the reading.

Writing Strategies

▶ Have students make a K-W-L chart for chapters as they read. After you preview the chapter, have them fill in the first column with what they know about the subject, and the second column with what they want to learn from the text. When they have finished reading, have them fill in the third column with what they learned.

► Have students use a T-chart (at the back of this guide) to contrast how the people of Mesopotamia did their work before and after various inventions. For example, have them contrast farming before and after the invention of the plow, or pottery-making before and after the invention of the potter's wheel.

Listening and Speaking Strategies

► To spark students' interest, read aloud the title and first paragraph of each chapter. Use the reading as a springboard for predicting what the chapter is about. Record and review students' predictions. When students have finished reading the chapter, ask whether their predictions were correct.

► Have volunteers read the Archaeologist at Work feature on pages 20–22 aloud to the class. Divide the feature into four or five sections, and have pairs of volunteers read the questions and answers as the interviewer and Glenn Schwartz. Coach students on how to read the text expressively.

UNIT VOCABULARY LIST

The following words that appear in Unit 1 are important for your students' understanding of the social studies content as well as for development of literacy. Use these words for vocabulary study or to reinforce language arts skills (e.g., synonyms, compound words, prefixes and suffixes, and related words). The words are listed below in the order in which they appear in the chapters.

Chapter 1	Chapter 2	Chapter 3	Chapter 4
tell	isolated	invention	bushel
findspot	course	disintegrate	token
specialist	lush	bronze	communication
remains	gazelle	cylinder	syllable
broiling	ammunition	sprawling	homonym
spearhead	obsidian	artisan	reed
	dedicated	remnants	syllabary
	canal	radioactive	cuneiform
	silt	plow	memorize
		technology	

ANCIENT TRASH AND BURIED TREASURE: ARCHAEOLOGISTS AT WORK

PAGES 16–22

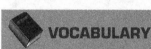
VOCABULARY

conservator person who tries to protect ancient objects found by archaeologists, sometimes treating the objects with special materials to keep them from falling apart

WRITING

- **Skit** Have students turn the story of Alice Petty's finding the tomb at Umm el-Marra into a skit showing her disappointment over not finding anything and then her elation over finding the tomb.

CHAPTER SUMMARY

In the Near East, most ancient remains are found in tells—mounds that can be many acres in extent, which are made up of the debris left of ancient towns. Archaeologists excavate these tells carefully in order to learn as much as possible about the people who lived there. Occasionally they find valuable objects, for example in tombs, but usually what they find is the trash that people left behind such as broken pots, pieces of bone, and worn grinding stones.

PERFORMANCE OBJECTIVES

- ▶ To understand what archaeologists do at their "digs"
- ▶ To analyze the stories that the remains of ancient civilizations tell
- ▶ To understand the special significance of the find at Umm el-Marra

BUILDING BACKGROUND

Before reading, elicit from students what they know about archaeological fieldwork, and where that knowledge comes from (movies and documentaries). Ask students what would be exciting if they were excavating an ancient city.

WORKING WITH PRIMARY SOURCES

Have students preview the pictures in the chapter. Explain that a "primary source" can be an object as well as a written source. Have students identify the primary sources in this chapter and predict what archaeologists are able to tell about the people who made them.

GEOGRAPHY CONNECTION

Region Have students study the map on pages 12–13. Have them find the sites mentioned in the chapter (Umm el-Marra, Terqa). Elicit from students the modern name of the region detailed on the map (*Middle East*), and ask them to name any Middle Eastern countries they know. (*Possible answers: Egypt, Israel, Lebanon, Syria, Turkey, Jordan, Saudi Arabia, Iraq, Iran, Kuwait, Palestinian Territories*) Explain that we identify these countries as a *region* for several reasons: the similarity of land features, climate, religion, and culture across the area. Perhaps also note that some countries that we include in the Middle East (such as Afghanistan and Libya) are generally not included in the ancient Near East.

READING COMPREHENSION QUESTIONS

1. What are archaeologists looking for in Near Eastern tells? (*They are looking for artifacts from ancient civilizations—pottery sherds, leftovers from ancient meals, broken walls, and other ancient "trash."*)
2. How do archaeologists decide which *tells* to excavate? (*They usually excavate the larger tells, or ones that are not covered by modern buildings.*)
3. Why do archaeologists call their findings "buried treasure? (*They call it buried treasure because of the stories it tells about the people who lived there, used the articles, and then threw them away.*)

4. Why is excavating a *tell* in the Near East such a challenging project? (*It is extremely hot in the daytime. The site is windblown and dirty. The work is exacting and time-consuming. The finds are usually not glamorous.*)

CRITICAL THINKING QUESTIONS

1. Archaeologists who work on a dig all have special jobs to do. What are those jobs? What might each archaeologist be able to learn about the past people from his or her special materials? (*Jobs: direct workmen, write down where each find is discovered, take photos, analyze plant remains, analyze pottery, analyze animal bones, conserve objects. Students should suggest what each type of remains might tell about the community.*)

2. Review the Archaeologist at Work feature on pages 20–22. How did Glenn Schwartz and his team come up with their theory of who the people buried in the tomb were and why those objects were buried with them? (*Students should describe the objects and skeletons found, the Mesopotamian texts they used for information, and their ability to date the remains.*)

3. Distribute copies of the blackline master for Chapter 1, and have students summarize and analyze Dr. Schwartz's findings at Umm el-Marra.

SOCIAL SCIENCES

Science, Technology, and Society   Have students research the tools and techniques used by archaeologists at their digs. One useful site is *www.socialstudiesforkids.com/articles/archaeology/archtools.htm*. Have students display pictures of the tools and archaeologists using them.

READING AND LANGUAGE ARTS

Reading Nonfiction   Have students read aloud the Archaeologist at Work feature on pages 20–22. Discuss students' reactions to the interview. Ask them what the interview adds and why it is useful in Chapter 1.

Using Language   Direct students to look at the second paragraph on page 19. Ask them to identify the personal pronouns in the paragraph and explain to whom each of the pronouns refers.

SUPPORTING LEARNING

English Language Learners   Read the definition of the noun *tell* (pages 16–17). Have students define the verb *tell* and discuss the authors' statement: "a tell . . . tells about the past." Encourage students to use both noun and verb in original sentences to show they understand the meanings.

Struggling Readers   Have students use the K-W-L graphic organizer (at the back of this guide) to identify the topics they would like to know more about.

EXTENDING LEARNING

Enrichment   Interested students can find more information about archaeologists' excavations at Umm el-Marra online at *www.jhu.edu/neareast/uem/*.

Extension   Have students create a skit based on the description of the archaeologist as time traveler (page 22). Students can role-play the archaeologist and the ancient people who used the things the archaeologist discovered. The ancient people can express their feelings about being remembered.

THEN and **NOW**

Terqa was a major city in ancient Mesopotamia, and was for some time a major commercial and governmental center. Not all of the tell is accessible to archaeologists, as some of it is covered by modern buildings.

LINKING DISCIPLINES

Art Have students make copies of the artifacts found in this and subsequent chapters. They can start an ancient Near East museum corner in the classroom with their copies.

NAME **DATE**

PLOTTING THE TOMB OF UMM EL-MARRA

Directions
Use the diagram to indicate where the different artifacts where found in the tomb at Umm el-Marra described in the Archaeologists at Work feature in Chapter 1. Then answer the questions in complete sentences.

TOMB AT UMM EL-MARRA

Level 1	Brick Box
Level 2	
Level 3	

1. How could the archaeologists tell that the women buried in the tomb were wealthy?

_____

_____

2. What made the archaeologists think that the men buried below the women were lower ranking than the women?

_____

_____

3. Why were valuable objects buried with these people?

_____

_____

NAME _____ **DATE** _____

A. MULTIPLE CHOICE

Circle the letter of the best answer to each question.

1. To an archaeologist, a tell is
   a. an ancient text.
   b. a well.
   c. a place where humans have lived.
   d. a hill.

2. The ancient city of Terqa was
   a. one of the largest cities in Syria.
   b. found near Umm el-Marra.
   c. destroyed by grave robbers.
   d. overlooked by archaeologitsts.

3. Archaeologists pinpoint the exact spot where an artifact is found at a dig to learn all of the following **except**
   a. how the object was used.
   b. the name of the person who used it.
   c. when the object was buried.
   d. when the object was thrown away.

4. Archaeologists rarely find things made of metal at a dig because
   a. these things were valuable and tended to be reused.
   b. ancient people did not know how to work with metals.
   c. ancient people did not consider metals very valuable.
   d. metal objects were not buried in tombs.

5. A conservator is an important member of an archaeological team because
   a. someone has to carry the artifacts.
   b. artifacts must be preserved for study.
   c. nobody likes the job.
   d. conserving water is important.

B. SHORT ANSWER

Write one or two sentences to answer each question.

6. How do archaeologists use pottery sherds to figure out when a tell was occupied?

_____

_____

7. Why are most things that archaeologists find made of bone, stone, or clay?

_____

_____

8. Why might an archaeologist feel like a time traveler while excavating a tell?

_____

_____

C. ESSAY

On a separate sheet of paper, write an essay telling why it is important for an archaeological team to be made up of experts in various areas.

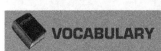

FOR HOMEWORK

STUDENT STUDY GUIDE

pages 13–14

VOCABULARY

domesticated describing animals that have been tamed for use by humans and that live in herds

irrigation bringing water to fields by artificial means: for example, canals and ditches

✎ WRITING

○ **Explanation** Have students use the picture on page 27 to write a paragraph explaining how ancient Mesopotamian farmers
○ made use of water from the Tigris and Euphrates rivers.

CHAPTER SUMMARY

The first villages in southern Mesopotamia were located near the rivers and marshes where people could grow their plants in the damp soil and fish. As the land grew drier people began to use irrigation agriculture, watering their crops by digging canals. Many of these ancient villages are now located in the desert because the courses of the rivers have changed. Few natural resources exist in southern Mesopotamia, so the people traded for stone to make their tools.

PERFORMANCE OBJECTIVES

▶ To understand the connection between irrigation and the growth of towns
▶ To recognize the importance of the rivers in Mesopotamia
▶ To analyze the beginnings of Mesopotamian culture

BUILDING BACKGROUND

Elicit students' knowledge of how rivers flood and the effects of flooding. Make sure they understand that a flood can have positive effects (leaving fertile soil), too. Explain that such flooding created a large area of fertile land in Mesopotamia.

WORKING WITH PRIMARY SOURCES

Discuss with students what they can learn about ancient Mesopotamia from the engraving on the trough on pages 24–25. (*Possible answers: that sheep were important to the Mesopotamians; that the building in the middle is very similar in shape and construction to the modern building in the illustration on page 26, showing that the same construction techniques have been used in southern Mesopotamia for thousands of years.*)

GEOGRAPHY CONNECTION

Location   Have students study the map on page 28. Have them use the mileage scale to determine how far the site of Eridu is from the Persian Gulf today. (*about 150 miles*) Elicit why Eridu is so far from the ocean now when it was so close to it 7,000 years ago. (*The Euphrates and Tigris rivers extended the land by dropping more soil downstream.*)

READING COMPREHENSION QUESTIONS

1. Why did most of the people of Mesopotamia live right next to the Tigris and Euphrates rivers? (*The climate was so hot and dry that people had to live on the riverbanks to be able to get enough water.*)
2. How did the people of Eridu get enough water to satisfy the needs of their growing population? (*They built levees to keep the river flowing near their settlement. They dug canals and ditches to irrigate their fields.*)
3. What drew different types of people to southern Mesopotamia? (*Farmers came for the fertile irrigated soil. Traders came to sell their goods in the towns that developed.*

4. What shrine was the town of Eridu built around? (*the shrine to Ea, the god of fresh water*)

CRITICAL THINKING QUESTIONS

1. Why did the people of Eridu build most things out of mud and clay? (*Those were the resources that they had. The wood that grew in the area—palm trees—was not useful for building.*)
2. How can archaeologists tell that Eridu was a lively trade center? (*They have found things there from far away: flint from northern Mesopotamia and obsidian from Turkey. These things must have been brought to Eridu by traders.*)
3. Distribute copies of the blackline master for Chapter 2 so students can diagram the causes of the development of towns in southern Mesopotamia.

SOCIAL SCIENCES

Civics   Irrigation ditches may have been one of the earliest forms of public works projects. Have students find pictures of levees and irrigation ditches on the Internet or in print sources to understand how much group effort is needed to build and maintain such things. Then have them evaluate why such a large project would require civic organization.

READING AND LANGUAGE ARTS

Reading Nonfiction   Have students read aloud the first two paragraphs of the chapter and discuss what they think will come next. After reading the chapter, ask students the purpose of starting the chapter with details about a modern person. Then have them identify the sentence that serves as a transition from the present to the past. (*Seashells in the desert?*)

Using Language   Point out the use of figurative language on page 23 (*wall of heat*) and the simile on page 24 (*Like a horse . . . reins.*) Define *simile* and discuss the difference between a simile and figurative language. Encourage students to use figurative language and similes in descriptions.

SUPPORTING LEARNING

Struggling Readers   Have students use the main idea map graphic organizer (see the reproducibles at the back of this guide) to help them understand the significance of the chapter topic. They can write *Growth of Towns* in a central circle, and the headings *Irrigation, Trade,* and *Domestication* in the surrounding circles. Students can then add details from the chapter to complete the map and show the connections among the circled topics.

EXTENDING LEARNING

Enrichment   Ask a group of students to investigate the current state of the Tigris and Euphrates rivers. Based on information in the chapter students can formulate questions about the rivers and seek out answers in print and online encyclopedias.

Extension   Invite students to create a three-dimensional model based on the illustration at the bottom of page 27 showing the river higher than the land around it and the way sweet water was tapped for irrigation.

LINKING DISCIPLINES

Science Students can research the most common use of levees in the United States today: flood control. Have students learn how levees are constructed and what happens when they fail.

THEN and NOW

Irrigation ditches and canals are still used throughout the Middle East to bring water to fields. Students can search the Internet for pictures of fields and irrigation ditches.

WHY TOWNS GREW IN MESOPOTAMIA

Directions

Complete the cause and effect chart with information from Chapter 2 to show how irrigation might have led to the growth of towns in southern Mesopotamia.

Because of This...	This Happened
The soil of southern Mesopotamia had no hard rocks to form river beds.	
The people of southern Mesopotamia built levees.	
Marshlands in southern Mesopotamia began to dry up.	
Families had more children and population grew.	
The canal system expanded.	
Southern Mesopotamia developed good farming conditions.	
Traders flocked to the growing villages in southern Mesopotamia to sell their wares.	
Temples to the gods were built in the towns in southern Mesopotamia.	

NAME   **DATE**

A. MULTIPLE CHOICE

Circle the letter of the best answer for each question.

1. In Mesopotamia, ancient peoples first settled in
    a. the south, near the Persian Gulf.   **c.** the north, in the cooler hills.
    b. the west, in the desert.   **d.** the east, near the Zagros Mountains.

2. The people of Eridu depended on the Euphrates River for all of the following **except**
    a. defense.   **c.** watering their crops.
    b. drinking water.   **d.** water for their herds.

3. The settlers of Eridu built their houses out of
    a. the wood of date trees.   **c.** mud, clay, and reeds.
    b. stone.   **d.** animal hides.

4. Once it was irrigated, the soil of southern Mesopotamia
    a. turned into unusable mud.   **c.** could be used to control floods.
    b. was not good for farming.   **d.** produced rich crops.

5. The lack of palaces in the lowest levels of the tell at Eridu means that the people
    a. could not construct large buildings.   **c.** were not rich enough to build palaces.
    b. did not have kings for many years.   **d.** were ruled by a democratic government.

B. SHORT ANSWER

Write one or two sentences to answer each question.

6. Why is the site of Eridu so far from water today?

_____

_____

7. How do we know that the people of Eridu were involved in trading?

_____

_____

8. Why were traders attracted to the towns of southern Mesopotamia?

_____

_____

C. ESSAY

Write an essay on a separate sheet of paper explaining the reasons why towns grew in southern Mesopotamia.

OF POTTERS AND POTS, PLOWME AND PLOWS: TECHNOLOGY AND THE FIRST CITIES

PAGES 29–35

 VOCABULARY

potter's wheel a flat wheel that can be spun to help shape clay into pottery

millennium a block of 1,000 years

colonists groups of people who leave their homes to create new communities elsewhere, carrying their traditions with them

 WRITING

○ **Travel Brochure**
Have students create a travel brochure for the city of Uruk. Students should include the temple complex, artisans' quarters, government center, trade centers, and living quarters of the rich and famous.

CHAPTER SUMMARY

The period from 3800 to 3100 BCE, known as the Uruk Period, was a time of great technological change in Mesopotamia. Innovations included the pottery wheel, the plow, the wheel (and hence the wagon), bronze-working, and cylinder seals. These innovations, allowed for the growth of the world's first cities, along with an increasing distinction between rich and poor. The people of the Uruk civilization also founded colonies throughout Mesopotamia and traded with regions as far away as Egypt.

PERFORMANCE OBJECTIVES

▶ To understand the qualities ascribed to civilizations
▶ To recognize the changes taking place in Mesopotamia

BUILDING BACKGROUND

Elicit from students the types of clay pottery their families use. Then have students imagine that there is no metal, glass, or plastic. What items would clay pots replace in their homes?

WORKING WITH PRIMARY SOURCES

Have students look at the picture of the ancient Mesopotamian potter's wheel on page 30. Elicit students' knowledge of making pottery, either with a wheel or by the coiled ropes of clay technique discussed in the text. Have students evaluate which technique would produce pots faster and which would produce stronger or more useful pots.

GEOGRAPHY CONNECTION

Interaction   Elicit from students that the Mesopotamians both depended on their environment (using the abundant clay to make pots for hundreds of uses) and adapted to their environment (developing bronze plows to break up the heavy clay soil for farming).

READING COMPREHENSION QUESTIONS

1. What were the earliest important innovations in Mesopotamian technology? (*potter's wheel, plow*)
2. Why was the development of bronze an important breakthrough? (*Bronze is a strong metal that could be used in many parts of life: plows, weapons, pitchers, jewelry.*)
3. Why do historians call the time around 3500 BCE in Mesopotamia the "Uruk period"? (*Uruk was one of the major cities of Mesopotamia at the time. It was a sprawling city of 10,000 people. Its remains are impressive, and show the development of a class system as well as a complex religion.*)
4. Distribute copies of the blackline master for Chapter 3 so students can trace the technological innovations in Mesopotamia at the time.

CRITICAL THINKING QUESTIONS

1. What effects did improved farming methods have on Mesopotamian life? (*The Mesopotamians could grow more food and feed more people. They could produce a surplus of crops that they could then trade for objects they desired.*)
2. Why is the existence of "professionals"—spinners, weavers, potters, metalworkers—in Mesopotamia an important step toward civilization? (*These professionals specialized in a certain work; they did not have to do everything for themselves. They had time to produce quality materials for trading purposes. Trading meant a more complex, farther-reaching society.*)
3. What aspects of civilization did the Mesopotamians of the Uruk period possess? (*cities, government, organized religion, specialized labor, long-distance trade, and a class system*)

SOCIAL SCIENCES

Economies   Have students brainstorm a list of specialists that exist in our modern economy. Ask: Why is having a specialized skill valuable to people? Discuss with students that specialists can do a certain job better than other people, and can get paid to do that work by others.

READING AND LANGUAGE ARTS

Reading Nonfiction   Invite students to look carefully at the graphic aids in the chapter and to evaluate how each one adds to their understanding of the chapter content. Ask questions such as: How do the images of the pots on page 29 help you understand ancient pottery technology?

Using Language   Have students identify the words on page 29 that introduce each step in the process of making a pot by hand. (*First, Then, Afterward*) Ask: What would be another way to identify these steps? (*number them, use bullets*) Then ask students to point out the verbs that describe the process (*rolled, coiled, made, painted, baked*). Students can then write sentences of their own describing a simple process.

SUPPORTING LEARNING

English Language Learners   After reading the explanation of *millennium* on page 32, have students define it in their own words. Make sure students understand why the 3000s BCE are called the fourth millennium BCE.

Struggling Readers   Have students use the outline graphic organizer (at the back of this guide) to identify the main topics and supporting details in the chapter.

EXTENDING LEARNING

Enrichment   Ask a group of students to learn more about carbon dating and present their findings to the class. Have them investigate methods used for dating non-animal or plant remains.

Extension   A group of students can create a skit based on the "Aha!" moment, described on page 32, when a someone first made the connection between a potter's wheel and a cart wheel. The skit can include roles for admiring townspeople who congratulate the visionary and discuss how wheeled vehicles could change their lives.

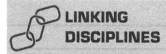

LINKING DISCIPLINES

Math Review with students that *millennium* means "1,000 years." Have students create a millennium timeline for the chapter, from 5000 BCE running through the BCE/CE divide, and up to the present. Ask them to mark the millennia on their timelines, and place the events in the chapter in the proper divisions. Have them identify the millennium in which each event occurred and how many millennia ago each event occurred.

THEN and **NOW**

The remains of Uruk are found approximately 160 miles south-southeast of Baghdad, near the city of Nasiriyah in modern Iraq.

INNOVATIONS IN ANCIENT MESOPOTAMIA

Directions
Complete the chart by explaining how each change in technology affected the lives of Mesopotamians in the fourth millennium BCE.

Innovation	Effects
Potter's wheels	
Plow	
Bronze	
Spinning and weaving	
Wheeled carts	
Cylinder seals	

NAME 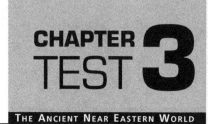 **DATE**

A. MULTIPLE CHOICE

Circle the letter of the best answer for each question.

1. The invention of the potter's wheel meant that potters could
   a. make larger pots.
   b. make many more pots.
   c. charge more money for their products.
   d. make more beautiful pots.

2. What did Mesopotamians of the fourth millennium trade for luxury goods?
   a. pottery
   b. bronze
   c. beautiful cloth
   d. copper

3. The development of the wheeled cart affected trade by increasing
   a. the variety of goods that were traded.
   b. the cost of long-distance trading.
   c. the amount of goods that one person could transport.
   d. the time it took to make wool robes.

4. A cylinder seal was used by ancient Mesopotamian traders to
   a. show the price of a product.
   b. advertise the product.
   c. decorate the product.
   d. identify the owner of the goods.

5. Mesopotamians probably set up colonies in far-off lands primarily to
   a. ease crowding in their homeland.
   b. show off their wealth.
   c. gain control over trade in the region.
   d. sell the luxury goods they produced.

B. SHORT ANSWER

Write one or two sentences to answer each question.

6. Why didn't potters who used potter's wheels have to spend much time farming?

_____

_____

7. Why was the discovery of how to make bronze so important to Mesopotamian farmers?

_____

_____

8. What elements of a civilization did the Mesopotamians have by 3500 BCE?

_____

_____

C. ESSAY

On a separate sheet of paper, write an essay explaining the importance of innovations in pottery-making and farming to the development of Mesopotamian civilization.

CHAPTER 4

HOW WORDS CHANGED THE WORLD: THE INVENTION OF WRITING

VOCABULARY

alkali (AL-kuh-lye) mineral salt found in soil and desert sand; can be used to make soap

WRITING

● **Letter** Have students imagine they are ancient Mesopotamian farmers, potters, weavers, or traders. Have them write letters to each other proposing business deals. Students should describe their products using strong adjectives and sensory words.

CAST OF CHARACTERS

Mebaragesi (may-BAH-rah-GAY-see) king of a Sumerian city-state around 2700 BCE; author of earliest known royal inscription

CHAPTER SUMMARY

To keep track of the people and the wealth of the new cities of the Uruk period, the Mesopotamians developed a system of writing. It has its roots in an ancient accounting system that used tokens to designate commodities. By 3200 BCE scribes were writing on clay tablets using pictures to express words. Soon the script became more schematic and expressive, as the signs could represent syllables. This system of writing, called cuneiform, was first used to write the Sumerian language.

PERFORMANCE OBJECTIVES

▶ To trace the development of a written language in Mesopotamia
▶ To understand the difference between a syllabary and an alphabet
▶ To identify the uses for written language in ancient Mesopotamia

BUILDING BACKGROUND

Read the first complete paragraph on page 42 to students, and ask them to brainstorm a list of things they read each day that they "barely notice" they are reading. Then have them imagine what their lives would be like if we did not have a written language.

WORKING WITH PRIMARY SOURCES

Have students find out more about the clay tokens from which Sumerian cuneiform is thought to have its origins. One source of information is *www.ancientscripts.com/cuneiform.html*. Students can make their own tokens.

GEOGRAPHY CONNECTION

Interaction Help students recognize that the use of clay as a medium for writing cuneiform was a function of the natural resources available to the Mesopotamians. Let students experiment with clay and a thin craft stick to make their own cuneiform tablets.

READING COMPREHENSION QUESTIONS

1. What was the first step toward "writing" in Mesopotamia? What was it used for? (*The first form of writing was clay tokens of various shapes. It was used to keep track of herds, crops, and other business items.*)
2. How did pictures come to represent ideas as well as things? (*The pictures could be used to represent verbs and adjectives as well as nouns, or could be combined with other words to represent ideas.*)
3. How did symbols come to represent sounds? (*Each Sumerian word was expressed with a particular sound, usually just one syllable. These syllables could be represented by the symbol, even in contexts where it didn't have anything to do with the object in the symbol.*)
4. What is the difference between a syllabary and an alphabet? (*In an alphabet each symbol stands for one consonant or one vowel. In a syllabary, each symbol stands for a whole syllable. You need more symbols to express all the words.*)

5. What was most Sumerian writing used for? (*Most of it was used to keep track of taxes, trade, and other business accounts. Scribes wrote contracts, lists of words, hymns, and inscriptions for kings. Much later, educated Mesopotamians used it to write letters.*)

CRITICAL THINKING QUESTIONS

1. Why was the idea of drawing pictures to represent things such a giant leap forward for writing? (*Now symbols, or ideas, stood for objects. If they could represent objects, they could represent ideas as well.*)
2. Why do you think that the ability to read and write wasn't more widespread amongst the people of Mesopotamia? (*The Sumerian syllabary had hundreds of symbols; examples in the chapter are very complex. Few people would have had the time to memorize and learn all these symbols. Most people did not go to school.*)
3. Why did cuneiform become the written language of choice for other peoples in the region? (*Although complicated, it was a useful system for sending messages, which was vital for trade in the region, and much more reliable than verbal instructions sent by messenger.*)
4. Distribute copies of the blackline master for Chapter 4 so students can learn more about Sumerian cuneiforms.

SOCIAL SCIENCES

Economics   Have students evaluate the importance of scribes to the Mesopotamian economy in the 4th and 3rd millenniums BCE. Make a three-column table on the board with the headings *Long-Distance Trade, Taxes,* and *Contracts.* Elicit the benefits of scribes for each area.

READING AND LANGUAGE ARTS

Reading Nonfiction   Read aloud pages 37–39. Elicit students' views on the effectiveness of repeating the example of the two brothers and a messenger to show the origins of written communication. Have students summarize the different forms of communication described on these pages.

Using Language   Have students read aloud the paragraph on homonyms, pages 39–40. Elicit English homonyms such as *pail/pale, right/write,* and have students use them in original sentences.

SUPPORTING LEARNING

Struggling Readers   Have students use the main idea map graphic organizer (see the reproducibles at the back of this guide) to help them understand the development of writing. They can print *Writing* in the central circle, and the headings *Tokens, Pictograms,* and *Cuneiform* in the surrounding circles. Students can then add details from the chapter to complete the map.

EXTENDING LEARNING

Enrichment   Have a group of interested students use information from the Further Reading page and the Websites page to present an illustrated report on cuneiform. They can also use the cuneiform chart on the blackline master for Chapter 4.

Extension   Have a group of students research and illustrate a comparison of Mesopotamian pictograms and Egyptian hieroglyphs. They can then role-play a panel of experts explaining the similarities and differences.

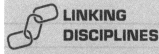

LINKING DISCIPLINES

Math Have students find out more about the Sumerian base-60 number system. One online source is *www.geocities. com/mathfair2002/ school/arit/arithm1.htm.*

THEN and **NOW**

Although the Sumerian syllabary was adopted by a number of peoples in the Near East, it later died out and was replaced by alphabets, which have fewer symbols. Have students find out about other syllabaries that are still used today, such as Chinese hanzi characters, Japanese kana syllabaries, the Cherokee syllabary, and the syllabaries of the Cree and Inuit peoples.

SUMERIAN CUNEIFORM WRITING

Directions

With a partner, study the cuneiform chart. On a separate sheet of paper, write words in English, including your name and the names of family members and friends. Then copy the cuneiform symbols that match the sounds in the words. If clay and a thin stick are available, you can make your own cuneiform tablets.

SOME CUNEIFORM SOUNDS AND SIGNS			
SOUND	**SIGN**	**SOUND**	**SIGN**
e		li	
el		mi	
ha		ni	
i		se	
ik		si	
ip		te	
is		ti	
ka		u	

NAME   **DATE**

A. MULTIPLE CHOICE

Circle the letter of the correct answer for each question.

1. The earliest form of record-keeping in Mesopotamia dates back as far as
  a. 1700 BCE.
  b. 2400 BCE.
  c. 3350 BCE.
  d. 8000 BCE.

2. Mesopotamian cuneiform signs were written by
  a. brushing ink on papyrus.
  b. drawing with chalk on slate.
  c. pressing a cut reed into clay.
  d. using a quill pen and paper.

3. Sumerian cuneiform signs started out as pictures and evolved into
  a. simpler symbols.
  b. beautiful artwork.
  c. complex diagrams.
  d. letters.

4. The Sumerian script is called a *syllabary* because each symbol usually represents a
  a. word.
  b. syllable.
  c. vowel.
  d. consonant.

5. Sumerian writing was complicated because
  a. each scribe wrote symbols differently.
  b. not everyone knew the language.
  c. there were more than 600 signs.
  d. no word lists existed.

B. SHORT ANSWER

Write one or two sentences to answer each question.

6. Describe what the first long-distance messages were like.

_____

_____

7. Because Mesopotamians had many homonyms in their language, how could they tell the meaning of a word?

_____

_____

8. What kinds of uses did Mesopotamian scribes find for writing?

_____

_____

C. ESSAY

Write an essay on a separate sheet of paper explaining in your own words how Mesopotamian pictograms became a useful written language.

Chapter 5	A World Full of Gods and Goddesses: Religion in Ancient Mesopotamia
Chapter 6	The Death of a Sumerian Lady: Queens, Kings, and Religion in Early Cities
Chapter 7	The First Superhero: The Story of Gilgamesh

UNIT OBJECTIVES

Unit 2 discusses the gods, religious practices, world view, and legends of the Mesopotamians. In this unit, your students will learn

► the Mesopotamians' relationship with their gods.
► the cozy world view of the Mesopotamians.
► what is known about the beginnings of kingship and the life of Mesopotamian royalty.
► the functions of government in Sumer. (It is never called Sumeria; the name of the land is Sumer.)
► the ideas found in *The Epic of Gilgamesh*.

PRIMARY SOURCES

Unit 2 includes excerpts from the following primary sources:

► "The Shamash Hymn," Iraq
► "Incantation Against Thunder," Iraq
► Speech "To Enlil," Iraq
► "Myth of Atrahasis," Iraq
► Sumerian King List, Iraq
► Royal inscription of Eannatum, Iraq
► Sin-leqe-unnini, *The Epic of Gilgamesh*

Pictures of artifacts from early Mesopotamian civilizations can also be analyzed as primary sources to learn more about Mesopotamian religion and legends:

► Engraving of Shamash, the sun god, on a cylinder seal
► "Myth of Atrahasis" written on a clay tablet
► Mesopotamian world map drawn on a clay tablet
► Puabi's headdress, Ur, Iraq
► Skull with gold jewelry, royal tomb, Ur, Iraq
► Relief sculpture of Eannatum's army
► Standard of Ur mosaic
► Carving of head of Humbaba
► Engraving of Gilgamesh killing Humbaba
► Engraved plaque showing a Mesopotamian banquet

BIG IDEAS IN UNIT 2

Gods, government, and **legends** are the big ideas presented in Unit 2. The unit opens with the genealogy of the Mesopotamian gods and the origins of humans, discusses the emergence of royalty in the Mesopotamian city-states, and describes the great epic about Gilgamesh, who is supposed to be one of the earliest kings of the great Sumerian city of Uruk. (The epic was not written in Sumerian, but Akkadian, so it is not a Sumerian epic.)

One way to introduce these ideas is to elicit what students know about myths and legends and what they tell us about a people's origins. Have students list popular elements of myths in their notebooks—gods, heroes, creation stories, fantastic beasts and amazing stunts, and so on. Remind students to look for these elements as they read the chapters of Unit 2.

GEOGRAPHY CONNECTION

Tell students that, at this time, the Mesopotamian people were not united into one state. Each major city constituted a separate state. Have them turn to the map on page 61, and note two divisions of Mesopotamia: Akkad, which is central Mesopotamia, and Sumer, or southern Mesopotamia. Stress that these were not political divisions, but rather divisions based on differences in language. The people of the two regions shared religious beliefs and other cultural characteristics. (The differences they have read about are between northern and southern Mesopotamia. Both Sumer and Akkad are in the southern half of Mesopotamia, so geographically they are pretty much the same—both are flat, arid river valleys.)

TIMELINE

2900 BCE	Kings begin to rule in southern Mesopotamia
2600 BCE	Legendary king Gilgamesh said to have ruled Uruk
2600 BCE	First royal inscription, by Mebaragesi, King of Kish
2500 BCE	Queen Puabi lived in Ur
2400 BCE	Royal inscription by Eannatum, King of Lagash
2100 BCE	Sumerian King List written
17th century BCE	"Myth of Atrahasis" written down
12th century BCE	*The Epic of Gilgamesh* written down

UNIT PROJECTS

Rereading *The Epic of Gilgamesh*

Have groups of students delve into a copy of *The Epic of Gilgamesh* to learn more about the major characters of the poem mentioned in the book: Gilgamesh, Enkidu, Humbaba, Ut-napishtim. See the Further Reading and Websites pages in the back of the student book for resources. Have students read lines describing these characters to the rest of the class so students can have a better understanding of the characters and of the language of the *Epic*.

Artwork

Have students sketch their own versions of the various gods discussed in Chapter 5. They can create a scene showing the gods acting like humans, as described in the chapter.

Research Report

Have partners investigate two of the Mesopotamian cities mentioned in Chapter 6: Kish and Ur. Have them create a visual display of each city, with either pictures of remains or drawings of the cities.

ADDITIONAL ASSESSMENT

For Unit 2, divide the class into groups and have them all undertake the Rereading the Epic of Gilgamesh project so that you can assess their understanding of Mesopotamian myths and what they say about what Mesopotamians believed in and the characteristics they valued. Use the scoring rubric at the back of this guide to assess students' work, and have students rate their own work with the self-assessment rubric.

UNIVERSAL ACCESS

The following strategies are designed to cover a range of learning styles and reading, language, and skill levels. You may find that any of your students will benefit from various strategies presented.

Reading Strategies

▶ To facilitate reading, review the reason for punctuation elements that students will encounter as they read. For example, for Chapter 5, explain that ellipses (…), as in the extracts, are used to indicate that the original text has been shortened.

▶ Remind students not to ignore unfamiliar words. Students can have their journals open as they read so they can jot down unfamiliar words and then look them up in a dictionary when they have finished the section.

▶ Have partners read the text silently together, and then review the main ideas and details when they are both finished.

Writing Strategies

▶ Have students make a two-column chart for each chapter that identifies individuals important to Mesopotamian religion and government. They should list the individuals in the left column and describe their functions in the right column.

▶ Students may enjoy inserting themselves as characters in *The Epic of Gilgamesh*. They should write a few lines in the style of the *Epic* describing themselves and their actions.

Listening and Speaking Strategies

▶ To set the stage for reading a chapter, tell students three or four questions that they can use to organize their reading. The questions can be keyed to sections of the chapter or to the main topics discussed. Students can write down the questions and take notes under each one.

▶ If reading a chapter aloud, have volunteers practice reading the excerpts from primary sources with expression. Then, when you reach each excerpt, have the volunteer stand and read it. Students could also do this in small groups.

UNIT VOCABULARY LIST

The following words that appear in Unit 2 are important for your students' understanding of the social studies content as well as for development of literacy. Use these words for vocabulary study or to reinforce language arts skills (e.g., synonyms, compound words, prefixes and suffixes, and related words). The words are listed below in the order in which they appear in the chapters.

Chapter 5	Chapter 6	Chapter 7
radiate	cosmetic	dismal
praise	loot	deathbed
pelt	headdress	immortality
crave	grindstone	consolation
reputation	attendant	epic
legend	minister	banquet
midwife	chariot	chorus
prosper	ziggurat	
neglect	inscription	
tablet	spoil	
envision	fortify	
hub	draft	
	legacy	
	priestess	

A WORLD FULL OF GODS AND GODDESSES: RELIGION IN MESOPOTAMIA

PAGES 43–48

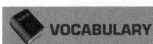 **VOCABULARY**

polytheists people who believe in many gods

incantation magic spell or charm

midwife woman who helps others in child-birth

 WRITING

○ **Poem** Have students imagine that they were ancient Mesopotamians and write their own poems of praise for a Mesopotamian god or goddess of their choosing, following the style of the poems in this chapter.

CHAPTER SUMMARY

The Mesopotamians had a polytheistic religion, in which the chief gods were believed to be the cosmic forces such as the sun (Shamash), the moon (Sin), the fresh water (Ea), and the storm (Adad). The king of the gods was Enlil and the goddess of war and love was Ishtar. These gods were responsible for all natural phenomena and even for the existence of humans, whom they created in order to serve them.

PERFORMANCE OBJECTIVES

▶ To identify the Mesopotamian gods and goddesses
▶ To retell the origin myths of the Mesopotamian gods and humans
▶ To understand the cozy world view of the Mesopotamians

BUILDING BACKGROUND

Have students tell legends that they know about gods and goddesses. Elicit from them a list of qualities of the gods they know about. Have them compare what they know with the characteristics of the Mesopotamian gods they will read about.

WORKING WITH PRIMARY SOURCES

Have students read the excerpt from "The Adoration of Inanna in Ur" in the *World in Ancient Times Primary Sources and Reference Volume* and analyze the way in which Mesopotamians viewed their gods.

GEOGRAPHY CONNECTION

Regions   The text refers to the approximate size of the world in the Mesopotamians' view—about 500 miles across. Have students contrast this with our modern conception of the world and universe. Then have them compare it to the size of your state, both in terms of distance and time it takes to travel that distance.

READING COMPREHENSION QUESTIONS

1. What character traits did the Mesopotamians give to Shamash, the sun god? *(He was believed to be immortal, and able to see everything. He was believed to be a judge who punished evildoers and rewarded those who lived good lives.)*
2. What did Mesopotamians believe was the cause of good and bad happenings on earth? *(Good things happened when the gods were happy; bad things happened when they were upset.)*
3. Who were the important Mesopotamian gods and goddesses, and what part of the universe did each control? *(Shamash was the sun god. Adad was the god of thunder and storms. Ishtar was the goddess of love and war. Enlil was the leader of the gods. Ea was the god of fresh water.)*

4. Why did the Mesopotamians believe that the universe was so small? (*They had no science, and rarely experienced anything beyond what they could see or visit from their homes. The farthest almost anyone traveled was about 500 miles.*)

CRITICAL THINKING QUESTIONS

1. Summarize in your own words the legendary events leading up to the creation of humans. (*Anu was the father of the gods. The first thing the gods did was separate Earth from sky. Then Enlil placed the stars and moon in the sky and created the Tigris and Euphrates rivers. The lesser gods became tired of working for Enlil, and rebelled. Ea saved the day by suggesting that a new creature—humans—be created. Humans were created by Mami from clay and the blood of a god.*)
2. Distribute copies of the blackline master for Chapter 5 so that students can analyze Mesopotamian writing about Inanna.

SOCIAL SCIENCES

Science, Technology, and Society Ask students to put themselves in the place of the ancient Mesopotamians. All they know about the world is what they see and what other local people tell them about the world. How would they envision the world and its size? What explanations would they give for human-made things or natural events that originate from outside their direct experience?

READING AND LANGUAGE ARTS

Reading Nonfiction Ask volunteers to read aloud the quotations from ancient writings in the chapter, including the Great Flood sidebar (page 44). Elicit students' reactions to the quotations and have them assess the value of including these quotes in the chapter.

Using Language Discuss the definition of *polytheists* (page 44). Point out that the prefix *poly-* is from the Greek *polus*, meaning "many." Have students use the dictionary to find definitions of other words with the prefix *poly-*: *polygamy, polygon, polyglot, polytechnic.* Have them use one or more of the words in an original sentence.

SUPPORTING LEARNING

Struggling Readers Have students create short "biographies" of the gods Shamash and Adad in their own words.

EXTENDING LEARNING

Enrichment Have a group of students dig deeper into the Mesopotamian gods at *www.mesopotamia.co.uk/gods/explore/exp_set.html,* a site recommended on the Websites page of their book. Students can prepare a presentation about the gods for the class.

Extension Invite students to practice and perform a reading of the songs to the gods on pages 43, 44, 45, and 47. They should read with expression and feeling.

LINKING DISCIPLINES

Science Have interested students investigate how modern scientists measure the size of the earth and other bodies in our solar system.

CAST OF CHARACTERS

Enheduanna (en-HEH-doo-AH-nah) high priestess of the moon god (24th century BCE); first known author in history

THEN and NOW

No one believes in the Mesopotamian gods any more. Most people who live in present-day Mesopotamia (the countries of Iraq and Syria) are Muslims who believe in one god, Allah.

ANALYZING A HYMN TO THE MESOPOTAMIAN GODDESS INANNA

Directions

Read the excerpt from the priestess Enheduanna's "Adoration of Inanna in Ur." Inanna (Ishtar) was the Mesopotamian goddess of love and war.

In the . . . battle, everything was struck down before you,
My queen, you are all devouring in your power,
You kept on attacking like an attacking storm,
Kept on blowing (louder) than the howling storm. . . .
My queen . . . the great gods,
Fled before you like fluttering bats,
Could not stand before your awesome face,
Could not approach your awesome forehead.
Who can soothe your angry heart! . . .
Queen, paramount in the land, who has (ever) paid you (enough) homage! . . .
The kingship of heaven has been seized by the woman Inanna,
At whose feet lies the flood-land.
That woman [Inanna] so exalted, who has made me tremble, together with the city of Ur
Stay her, let her heart be soothed by me. . . .

"You are known, you are known"—it is not of Nanna [the moon god] that I have recited it, it is of you that I have recited it.
"You are known by your heaven-like height,
You are known by your earth-like breadth,
You are known by your destruction of rebel-lands,
You are known by your massacring their people,
You are known by your devouring their dead like a dog,
You are known by your fierce countenance.
. . . You are known by your flashing eyes.
. . . You are known by your many triumphs"—
It is not of Nanna that I have recited it, it is of you that I have recited it.

1. What type of event does Enheduanna seem to be describing?

_____

2. What was the outcome of this event?

_____

3. How does Enheduanna say that Inanna is known?

_____

_____

4. How do you think the priestess Enheduanna plans to soothe Inanna's heart?

_____

_____

NAME   **DATE**

A. MULTIPLE CHOICE

Circle the letter of the best answer for each question.

1. The Mesopotamians believed that humans had been created for the purpose of
   a. ruling the earth.
   b. creating beautiful pottery.
   c. feeding, clothing, and sheltering the gods.
   d. turning deserts into fertile land.

2. Mesopotamians believed that during thunderstorms,
   a. the gods were laughing at humans.
   b. the gods were happy with humans.
   c. Adad and Shamash were fighting.
   d. Enlil and Ishtar were fighting.

3. Mesopotamians would have been especially concerned about keeping the god Ea happy because they depended on Ea for
   a. fresh water.
   b. sunlight.
   c. seeds.
   d. trade.

4. The universe to Mesopotamians included all of the following **except**
   a. the Upper and Lower Seas.
   b. a mythical land beyond the seas.
   c. the land of Mesopotamia.
   d. the Tigris and Euphrates rivers.

5. The Mesopotamians believed that the sun and the stars
   a. were put in place by the god Sin.
   b. stayed in the same position every day.
   c. moved around the earth.
   d. moved around the moon.

B. SHORT ANSWER

Write one or two sentences to answer each question.

6. What did the Mesopotamians think was the cause of good and bad things?

_____

_____

7. What did the Mesopotamians believed caused the gods to become unhappy with their leader, Enlil?

_____

_____

8. What did the Mesopotamians believe would happen if they served the gods well?

_____

_____

C. ESSAY

On a separate sheet of paper, write an essay summarizing why the Mesopotamians had such a "cozy" world view.

THE DEATH OF A SUMERIAN LADY: QUEENS, KINGS, AND RELIGION II EARLY CITIES

PAGES 49–54

FOR HOMEWORK

STUDENT STUDY GUIDE
pages 21–22

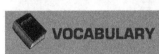

VOCABULARY

raw materials natural materials, such as wood, metals, and precious stones, from which other things are made

reign length of time that a ruler is in power

drafted forced to work

WRITING

Instructions Have students write a list of things that a Mesopotamian king might tell an assistant in charge of public works to do in a year. Students should prioritize the projects and use time order words to express which should be done first, next, and last.

CHAPTER SUMMARY

Around 2900 BCE the first kings began to rule city-states in Mesopotamia. Each city had its own government, which recruited workmen to build monumental structures, soldiers to fight against enemy neighbors, and workers to farm the palace lands. Scribes kept track of these activities on cuneiform tablets. The royal tombs at Ur show the wealth of these early Sumerian cities and the fact that they were trading with distant lands. Women had many freedoms and rights in the early city-states, and queens and priestesses played important roles in governing.

PERFORMANCE OBJECTIVES

► To understand the conclusions about Sumerian life made from evidence in the tomb of Puabi
► To learn about the rise of kings who ruled Sumerian cities
► To explain how Sumerian cities were becoming richer, better organized, and more warlike

BUILDING BACKGROUND

Have students imagine they are all-powerful kings and queens of a Sumerian city. Have them write a testimonial to themselves that they expect would be read by people hundreds of years later. What would they say about themselves?

WORKING WITH PRIMARY SOURCES

There are numerous translations of the Sumerian King List available online. One site is *www.geocities.com/protoillyrian/sumerian*. Have students read the list and compare the information to the map on pages 12–13 to get an idea of the seats of power of the rulers. Have them draw conclusions about the length of the earliest king's reigns compared with the length of the later king's reigns. (*The lengths of the early reigns were completely fictional.*)

GEOGRAPHY CONNECTION

Region   Have students draw conclusions as to why historians think of the ancient Near East of this time as a region rather than as specific states. (*The city-states were not unified, but the people in all the city-states had a shared religion, language, architectural style, pottery, writing system, and jewelry.*)

READING COMPREHENSION QUESTIONS

1. How did archaeologists know that Puabi was a wealthy, powerful woman, and perhaps a queen? (*She was buried with magnificent jewelry and other objects. Other people were buried with her. She is referred to as nin—"queen"—in her cylinder seal.*)
2. What do the gold and silver objects in Puabi's tomb say about trade in Mesopotamia at that time? (*Since there are no gold or silver mines in Mesopotamia, the people there must have had long-distance trading connections to other places.*)

3. How much territory did the early kings of Mesopotamia control? (*The kings controlled a city and the land around it. No king controlled all of the land.*)
4. What evidence is there that the leaders of Sumerian cities hired local people to work on projects such as city walls and gates, temples, and canals? (*Cuneiform tablets list the workers' names, their days of service, and the amount of barley each one was given.*)

CRITICAL THINKING QUESTIONS

1. Why would kings want to convince the Sumerians that the gods approved of them? (*Sumerians felt that gods controlled all aspects of life. If they believed the gods approved of the king, they would be more likely to support that king.*)
2. Study the picture of Eannatum's soldiers and the caption on page 53. What conclusions can you draw about Eannatum's army? (*The identical weapons and matching helmets and shields indicate that the government provided them. The formation marching show that these soldiers were highly trained. They seem to be a professional army.*)
3. Distribute copies of the blackline master for Chapter 6 so students can draw conclusions about Sumerian society based on the evidence in Puabi's tomb.

SOCIAL SCIENCES

Civics   Have students try to figure out why the inhabitants of Sumerian cities would work on projects like temples, canals, and walls (besides being paid for their work). Elicit that public works projects like these, although they may not benefit a person immediately, make the city a better place to live, and so people are willing to work on them or pay for them through taxes.

READING AND LANGUAGE ARTS

Reading Nonfiction   Invite students to read aloud the sidebars in this chapter. Then have students comment on each one and list questions it raises. Assign groups of students to find answers to the questions by researching the topics covered in each of the sidebars.

Using Language   Ask a volunteer to read aloud the quote from Leonard Woolley at the bottom of page 49. Elicit that the words in brackets were added by the textbook authors, replacing Woolley's original words, to make the quote understandable.

SUPPORTING LEARNING

English Language Learners   Have students define the words *excavate* and *excavation*. Discuss the derivation of the word, from Latin *ex* (*out*) and *cavare* (*to hollow*). Encourage students to use the words in original sentences.

Struggling Readers   Have students use the sequence of events graphic organizer (at the back of this guide) to put the chapter topics—the growth of trade, Sumerian city-states, and rule by kings—in chronological order.

EXTENDING LEARNING

Enrichment   Have a group research and report on Leonard Woolley's excavation of Ur, using *www.mesopotamia.co.uk/tombs/story/page01.html*.

Extension   Ask a group to create a list of questions they would like to ask Leonard Woolley about his discovery of Puabi's tomb. Students can write or create an oral presentation of their questions.

LINKING DISCIPLINES

Art Have students find online pictures of the materials from Puabi's tomb as well as the other royal tombs of Ur. The website *www. museum.upenn.edu* has many pictures. Students can copy the pictures and make a display of the treasures.

CAST OF CHARACTERS

Puabi (poo-AH-bee) Sumerian queen (around 2500 BCE whose burial was the richest of the royal tombs of Ur

Eannatum (ay-AH-nah-tum) king of Lagash around 2400 BCE

NAME

DATE

DRAWING CONCLUSIONS FROM PUABI'S TOMB

Directions

Complete the chart by explaining what each find in Puabi's tomb tells us about the society of Ur around 2500 BCE.

Discovery	What It Means
Gold and silver objects	
Cylinder seal with the words *Puabi, nin*	
Puabi's good teeth	
Skeletons found in slumped positions	

NAME _____ **DATE** _____

A. MULTIPLE CHOICE

Circle the letter of the best answer for each question.

1. Puabi's tomb was an important find because it
   a. was the first Sumerian tomb to be found.
   b. was found by Leonard Woolley.
   c. had not been disturbed by grave robbers.
   d. was filled with cuneiform tablets.

2. The presence of gold and silver objects in Puabi's tomb shows that
   a. Ur had trade contacts with faraway lands.
   b. she had a special liking for those metals.
   c. there were gold and silver mines in Mesopotamia.
   d. Mesopotamians did not know how to make gold and silver jewelry.

3. We can tell that the Sumerian King List is not completely factual because it
   a. misspells some ruler's names.
   b. says some kings reigned for thousands of years.
   c. was meant to be a legend passed down through generations.
   d. was inscribed in cuneiform on clay tablets.

4. The kings of this time typically ruled
   a. all of southern Mesopotamia.   **c.** several major cities.
   b. all the land of Mesopotamia.   **d.** a major city and its surrounding land.

5. In order to build city walls and other large projects, kings probably
   a. had the army do the work.   **c.** asked each family to do part of the job.
   b. drafted residents to do the work. **d.** had thousands of slaves do the work.

B. SHORT ANSWER

Write one or two sentences to answer each question.

6. What was Puabi's probable position in Ur?

_____

_____

7. How do archaeologists believe Puabi's servants followed her into the afterlife?

_____

_____

8. What do scholars think is one way that kings began to rule in southern Mesopotamia?

_____

_____

C. ESSAY

Write an essay on a separate sheet of paper giving reasons why having kings would be useful to the Sumerian cities.

CHAPTER 7

THE FIRST SUPERHERO: THE STORY OF GILGAMESH

STUDENT STUDY GUIDE

pages 23–24

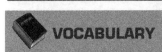 **VOCABULARY**

flood Mesopotamia experienced huge floods in ancient times, some of which may have seemed to have covered their "whole Earth"

king leader of a people

CAST OF CHARACTERS

Gilgamesh (GIL-guh-mesh) king of Uruk around 2600 BCE whose legendary adventures are recorded in the *Epic of Gilgamesh*

Enkidu (EN-kee-doo) legendary best friend of Gilgamesh

Sin-leqe-unnini (SIN LAY-kay oo-NEE-nee) 12th century BCE scribe who wrote the *Epic of Gilgamesh*

Ut-napishtim (oot-nah-PISH-tim) legendary Mesopotamian involved in flood myth

CHAPTER SUMMARY

The story of Gilgamesh is the earliest known epic poem. It was first written down in the early 2nd millennium BCE, but the best-preserved version was written in the 12th century. In the epic, the hero Gilgamesh and his friend Enkidu first battle monsters and divine beings but, after Enkidu's death, Gilgamesh sets out on a quest to find eternal life. Although he fails in his mission, the epic includes many important messages, such as the importance of enjoying life. The epic was probably originally performed for audiences by storytellers or singers.

PERFORMANCE OBJECTIVES

▶ To analyze the character of Gilgamesh
▶ To use legends to understand what was important to the Sumerian people

BUILDING BACKGROUND

Read the title of the chapter aloud, and elicit students' conceptions of a superhero. (*wears a uniform, has super powers, lives under a secret identity, battles master criminals*) Then have them state what a superhero from 4,600 years ago might be like.

WORKING WITH PRIMARY SOURCES

Have students read the excerpt from *The Epic of Gilgamesh* in *The World in Ancient Times Primary Sources and Reference Volume*. Discuss with them what this excerpt might say about Mesopotamian people's desires in life.

GEOGRAPHY CONNECTION

Place   One of the sidebars on page 57 refers to ancient floods in Mesopotamia and the echoes of such floods in *The Epic of Gilgamesh*. Have students investigate the ancient Mesopotamian floods and report to the class on their effects.

READING COMPREHENSION QUESTIONS

1. What did Gilgamesh do that made the gods angry? (*After he killed the monster Humbaba, the goddess Ishtar fell in love with him. He rejected and insulted her. Ishtar's father, Anu, sent the Bull of Heaven to punish Gilgamesh, but Gilgamesh killed the bull. The gods felt that humans were not supposed to have such power.*)
2. How did the gods get their revenge on Gilgamesh? (*They put a curse on his friend Enkidu. After Enkidu died, Gilgamesh began a life of wandering, trying to find immortality.*)
3. What ideas about humanity and the world does the story of Gilgamesh address? (*The story is concerned with what makes a hero, why people die, what is the meaning of friendship, and how to best live our lives.*)

4. Distribute copies of the blackline master for Chapter 7 to help students organize the information in the chapter.

CRITICAL THINKING QUESTIONS

1. Why would the fate of Gilgamesh after he killed the Bull of Heaven make sense to Mesopotamians? (*Mesopotamians believed that the gods rewarded humans for good behavior and punished them for bad behavior in this life. Challenging the gods the way Gilgamesh did was certainly bad behavior, so having to wander the world chasing an impossible dream would be a fitting fate.*)
2. Can you think of other stories in which a hero faces difficult challenges and sometimes acts in ways that don't seem very heroic? How are these stories similar to or different from the epic of Gilgamesh? (*Students might mention Star Wars, Lord of the Rings, Harry Potter—one thing that they share is that the hero is very human and has to overcome, or learn to live with, weaknesses.*)
3. Besides being an exciting story, what benefit would Mesopotamians get from listening to *The Epic of Gilgamesh* retold through the generations? (*For example, all Mesopotamians would be able to cherish their shared past.*)

SOCIAL SCIENCES

Civics   Review with students the benefits to a society of having shared legends and beliefs. Ask: What shared legends or beliefs do Americans have? Elicit the belief in our democratic institutions as well as popular folk myths or tall tales that tell something about the American character.

READING AND LANGUAGE ARTS

Reading Nonfiction   Have students respond to the chapter title by predicting what the story of Gilgamesh is about. After reading the chapter, ask students to evaluate the title and first sentence and decide whether "superhero" is a good description of Gilgamesh.

Using Language   Have students investigate the definitions and origins of these words found in the chapter: *epic, hero, immortality*. They can present the results of their research to the class.

SUPPORTING LEARNING

Struggling Readers   Have students use the sequence of events chart (see the reproducibles at the back of this guide) to summarize the adventures of Gilgamesh.

EXTENDING LEARNING

Enrichment   Interested students can find a translation of the end of the Gilgamesh epic at *http://alexm.here.ru/mirrors/www.enteract.com/jwalz/Eliade/159.html*, a link from a website (Internet Ancient History Sourcebook) recommended on the Websites page of their book. Students can prepare a choral reading of a section, such as Gilgamesh's conversation with Ut-napishtim.

Extension   Invite groups to create skits based on one or more scenes from the Gilgamesh story.

LINKING DISCIPLINES

Science Have students investigate more modern floods, such as the Johnstown flood in Pennsylvania in 1889, or the flooding in the Mississippi River basin in 1993, or recent floods in your state. Amazing statistics on the 1993 floods can be found online at *www.greatriver.com/FLOOD.htm*. Have students make displays showing the aftermath of such floods.

WRITING

Narrative Have students write a story based on the Gilgamesh epic. They should add dialogue between the characters.

NAME   **DATE**

WHAT MESOPOTAMIANS LEARNED FROM GILGAMESH

Directions

Complete the organizer by writing the answers to the four questions that appear at the end of the chapter. Base your answers on the story of Gilgamesh and what you have learned about the Mesopotamian people.

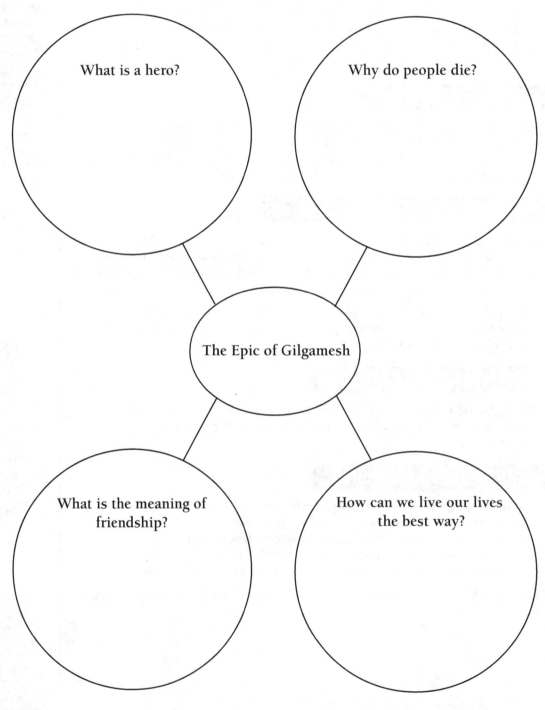

What is a hero?

Why do people die?

The Epic of Gilgamesh

What is the meaning of friendship?

How can we live our lives the best way?

A. MULTIPLE CHOICE

Circle the letter of the best answer for each question.

1. When Gilgamesh was a young man, he was
   a. a responsible adult.
   b. wise and careful.
   c. very ill.
   d. wild and self-centered.

2. Gilgamesh wanted to kill Humbaba so that he would be
   a. famous.
   b. safe.
   c. beloved.
   d. useful.

3. Gilgamesh spent a lifetime wandering the earth looking for a way to
   a. bring his friend Enkidu back to life.
   b. escape death.
   c. end the Euphrates River floods.
   d. conquer Uruk's enemies.

4. During Gilgamesh's travels, he was given a test by Ut-napishtim, and learned that he was
   a. immortal.
   b. the lost king of Uruk.
   c. an ordinary mortal.
   d. the favorite of the gods.

5. When Gilgamesh returned to Uruk, he realized that he could be
   a. content with mortal life.
   b. the greatest hero in the world.
   c. the best king of Uruk.
   d. happy to travel the world again.

B. SHORT ANSWER

Write one or two sentences to answer each question.

6. What did the Mesopotamians believe about the afterlife?

_____

_____

7. How was the story of Gilgamesh kept alive for 1,500 years before being written down?

_____

_____

8. What did Ut-napishtim do to deserve the gift of immortality from the god Enlil?

_____

_____

C. ESSAY

On a separate sheet of paper, write an essay telling how his experiences changed Gilgamesh.

UNIT OBJECTIVES

Unit 3 discusses the first Mesopotamian empire built by Sargon of Akkad, and the legal structures of the early Mesopotamian empires. In this unit, your students will learn

► how Sargon subdued all of Mesopotamia from the Mediterranean Sea to the Persian Gulf.
► the place of priests and priestesses in Mesopotamian society.
► the early law codes of Shulgi and Hammurabi.
► how Mesopotamian contracts and courts operated.

PRIMARY SOURCES

Unit 3 includes excerpts from the following primary sources:

► "The Legend of Sargon"
► Royal inscriptions of Sargon
► Letter from Ebla palace steward
► "The Curse of Agade"
► Enheduanna, "Hymn to Inanna"
► List of omens
► "I Will Praise the Lord of Wisdom"
► Shulgi, "Hymn to Himself"
► Shulgi, Prologue to the Laws
► Shulgi, Laws
► "The Wedding of the Amurru"
► Laws of Hammurabi
► Adoption contract from Iraq
► Adoption contract from Syria
► Inheritance claim

Pictures of Mesopotamian artifacts from this time period can also be analyzed as primary sources:

► Bronze bust of Mesopotamian king
► Sumerian-Eblaite dictionary tablet
► Monument of King Naram-Sin's victory
► Engraving of Enheduanna on alabaster disk, Ur
► Marble head of goddess
► Prayer statues

- ▶ Bronze image of King Shulgi
- ▶ Ziggurat of Ur
- ▶ Relief sculpture of Hammurabi and Shamash from the top of the law stela
- ▶ Bronze praying figure, perhaps of Hammurabi
- ▶ Contract with clay envelope
- ▶ Cylinder seal and its impression
- ▶ Relief sculpture of businessmen

BIG IDEAS IN UNIT 3

Empires, laws, and **religion** are the big ideas presented in Unit 3. The unit focuses on the developing civic institutions in Mesopotamia: the empire built by Sargon, the laws of Shulgi and Hammurabi, the role of priests and priestesses, and the workings of the legal system.

You can introduce these ideas by defining an institution as an established, respected organization in a society. Brainstorm a list of such institutions in the United States: government, religions, schools, and so on. Discuss the functions of each institution, and how they benefit society.

GEOGRAPHY CONNECTION

Have students look at the map on page 61 and trace the boundaries of Sargon's empire. Elicit that, although this was the first empire in history, it still remained within reach of the Tigris and Euphrates rivers. Have students explain the importance of rivers to settlement in the pre-modern era. Elicit that the empire didn't include lands to the east and west of the rivers because of geographical factors. Ask students to do research to find out why these areas were not settled, using the world atlas listed in the Further Reading section in their books.

TIMELINE

2340 BCE	Sargon comes to power in Akkad
2300 BCE	Sargon conquers all of Mesopotamia
2300 BCE	Kingdom of Ebla (in Syria) destroyed
2300 BCE	Enheduanna, Sargon's daughter, becomes priestess of the moon god (Nanna) at Ur
2094 BCE	King Shulgi comes to power in Mesopotamia
2000 BCE	"Curse of Agade" written
2000 BCE	Amorites invade Mesopotamia; Third Dynasty of Ur collapses
1792 BCE	Hammurabi comes to power in Babylon
1763 BCE	Hammurabi conquers much of Mesopotamia
1755 BCE	Hammurabi issues laws and has them carved in stone

UNIT PROJECTS

Twenty Questions

Assign partners different personalities (both human and god) from this unit: Sargon, Tira-il, Ibubu, Enheduanna, Nanna, Ea, Enlil, Shulgi, Hammurabi, Shamash, Samsu-iluna, Ninshubur-tayar, Patiya, and Shamash-nasir. Partners should find information in this unit or in prior chapters about their assigned personality. Then have the class play Twenty Questions to guess the personalities, with one of the partners representing the personality and the other acting as an assistant to answer the questions.

Law Monument

Have small groups find more information about the surviving laws of Hammurabi. They can use the online source listed on the Websites as well as print resources. Have students make their own cardboard monuments with some of the laws written on the monument.

Judging Mesopotamian Cases

Have groups of five or six students make up cases that have to be resolved by Mesopotamian judges. Two students in each case should be the judges, two should be the contending people, and one or two should be the witnesses. Groups can act out their cases before the rest of the class. Groups should prepare a contract, and should deliver their testimony before the judges and before Shamash. Encourage students to act expressively, perhaps indicating a fear of Shamash or some other mannerisms that will help the judges decide the case.

ADDITIONAL ASSESSMENT

For Unit 3, divide the class into groups and have them all undertake the Judging Mesopotamian Cases project so you can assess their understanding of the Mesopotamian justice system at the time of Hammurabi. Use the scoring rubric at the back of this guide to assess students' work, and have students rate their own work with the self-assessment rubric.

UNIVERSAL ACCESS

The following strategies are designed to cover a range of learning styles and reading, language, and skill levels. You may find that any of your students will benefit from various strategies presented.

Reading Strategies

▶ To facilitate reading, preview the photographs in each chapter so that students will be aware of the subject of the text.
▶ Ask students to read their books aloud at home to family members. If oral reports are assigned, remind them to practice once or twice before an audience at home so they can do their best work in class.

Writing Strategies

▶ Have students put themselves in the place of the people studied in this unit. Ask them to write journal entries representing daily activities for these people.
▶ Have groups of students write skits involving people from several of the chapters in the unit.

Listening and Speaking

▶ To spark students' interest, state facts from the chapter that are diametrically opposed to students' life experiences. Have them read to understand the context of such statements.

▶ Have students read a chapter in small groups, with each group member taking a turn reading while the other students take notes. Group members should then cooperate on an outline of the important points of the chapter.

UNIT VOCABULARY LIST

The following words that appear in Unit 3 are important for your students' understanding of the social studies content as well as for development of literacy. Use these words for vocabulary study or to reinforce language arts skills (e.g., synonyms, compound words, prefixes and suffixes, and related words). The words are listed below in the order in which they appear in the chapters.

Chapter 8	Chapter 9	Chapter 10	Chapter 11
waterproof	capital	dynasty	contract
laborer	alabaster	donation	witness
reign	cult	evidence	abandon
exaggeration	precious	verdict	estate
flax	glorify	barbarian	inherit
scribe	purification	assault	testimony
emphasize	diviner	accusation	oath
translation	constellation	foundation	
fragment	deformity		
territory	preside		
scribe	cathedral		
	mosque		

THE WORLD'S FIRST EMPIRE BUILDER: SARGON, KING OF AKKAD

PAGES 59–64

CAST OF CHARACTERS

Sargon (SAR-gon) king of Akkad who built the world's first empire

Ibubu (ih-BOO-boo) steward of the palace at Ebla (2400 BCE)

Tira-il (TEE-rah-eel) scribe at Ebla whose letter is earliest known example of diplomacy (2400 BCE)

Naram-Sin (NAH-rahm-SIN) king (2260–2223 BCE) of Akkadian Empire; grandson of Sargon; saw himself as divine

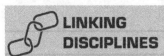

LINKING DISCIPLINES

Civics Have students learn more about the role of modern diplomats. Students can investigate the functions of the U.S. State Department or of the United Nations. Have students create a visual display showing what diplomats do.

CHAPTER SUMMARY

In the 24th century BCE, Sargon built the world's first empire when he united all of Mesopotamia and Syria under his rule. Documents from his reign show that he encouraged trade with regions as far away as the Indus Valley and organized the government of his empire, but he was remembered in later centuries mostly for his military victories. The site of Ebla, in Syria, provides the best documentation of this period of history in the many thousands of tablets that have been found there, which include the earliest known dictionary.

PERFORMANCE OBJECTIVES

▶ To explore the building of the first empire
▶ To understand diplomacy in the time of Sargon

BUILDING BACKGROUND

Ask students what empires they know about, such as the British, Roman, or Chinese empires. Elicit that an empire is a larger state than a country: it usually includes a number of different people and countries. Ask what challenges the rulers have in trying to hold together many peoples who speak different languages and have varied traditions. Have them speculate how much harder it would be to rule an empire without modern technologies such as telephone, fax, or email. Students can use a K-W-L chart (at the back of this guide) to help them organize their thoughts.

WORKING WITH PRIMARY SOURCES

"The Legend of Sargon" is available in translation at various places online: one such site is *www.fordham.edu/halsall/ancient/2300sargon1.html*. Have students read the legend (very little of it remains) to learn more about the myth that surrounded Sargon's origins.

GEOGRAPHY CONNECTION

Regions   Have students look at the map on page 61. Have them identify the approximate site of Agade, Sargon's capital. Then have them use the mileage scale to assess the size of the empire. *(approximately 900 miles from Lower Sea to Upper Sea, and about 300 miles across at its widest point)* Have students relate the size of Sargon's empire to the size of your state.

READING COMPREHENSION QUESTIONS

1. Where did Sargon come from? *(Since his native language was Akkadian, he probably grew up in Akkad, north of Sumer.)*
2. What cities did Sargon conquer to create his empire? *(The map on page 61 shows Ebla, Mari, Kish, Uruk, Lagash, and Ur as part of the empire. Agade was Sargon's capital. The quote from his royal inscription also mentions that he conquered Yarmuti.)*

3. What did the tablets found at Ebla tell archaeologists about relations between rulers at that time? (*Kings had representatives at the courts of foreign rulers. They sent instructions to the representatives by messenger. These representatives acted as diplomats, speaking for the king and presenting gifts.*)

4. Distribute copies of the blackline master for Chapter 8 so students can organize the information in the chapter.

CRITICAL THINKING QUESTIONS

1. What might the palace of Ebla looked like? How can you tell? (*The palace would have been full of gold, silver, and other valuable objects and adornments. We can tell this because so many people received payment from the king to make goods for the palace.*)

2. What do you think was the driving force behind the creation of Sargon's empire? Was it desire to control trade and wealth, protection from invaders, or something else? Give evidence for your answer. (*Possible answer: It was probably to control trade and wealth. Sargon conquered the cities along popular trade routes, and controlled the natural resources in the north.*)

SOCIAL SCIENCES

Economics   Help students understand the benefits to Sargon of controlling the mines and forests to the north as well as the trade routes between the Mediterranean Sea and Persian Gulf. Elicit that he would be able to get wood and minerals inexpensively, since they would be sent as tribute or taxes, and would get a share of the taxes charged traders passing through the empire's cities.

READING AND LANGUAGE ARTS

Reading Nonfiction   Invite students to examine the graphic aids in the chapter (illustrations and map), and assess how each one adds to the chapter.

Using Language   Have students identify the possessive pronouns in the last paragraph on page 60 (*its*). Have students explain the difference between *its* (possessive) and *it's* (contraction of *it is*).

SUPPORTING LEARNING

English Language Learners   Have small groups talk about Sargon. Have them differentiate fact from legend in the story of Sargon, and then report their findings to the class.

Struggling Readers   Have students use the main idea map graphic organizer (at the back of this guide) to help them understand Sargon's empire-building. They can write *Empire* in the central circle, and the headings *Trade, War,* and *Communication* in the surrounding circles, then add details from the chapter.

EXTENDING LEARNING

Enrichment   Invite a group of students to compare Sargon's empire to empires in other cultures. What elements do all empires have in common? How do they differ? Students can present their findings to the class.

Extension   Have students prepare a retelling and choral reading of the legend of Sargon using information and excerpts quoted in the chapter and a translation of the legend on the Internet Ancient History Sourcebook website: *www.fordham.edu/halsall/ancient/2300sargon1.html.*

VOCABULARY

empire a state that includes people of many nationalities, different languages, and different traditions ruled by one person

equids horses and horselike animals, such as mules and donkeys

diplomat a person who represents a ruler of one country in foreign lands and is empowered to act for that ruler

WRITING

Journal Have students write a journal entry for a day in the life of a diplomat at the time of Sargon's empire. Entries should include meetings with foreign rulers or discussions with conquered cities about what the emperor wants.

NAME   **DATE**

SARGON'S EMPIRE

Directions

Use the diagram to organize the information in Chapter 8 about Sargon's empire.

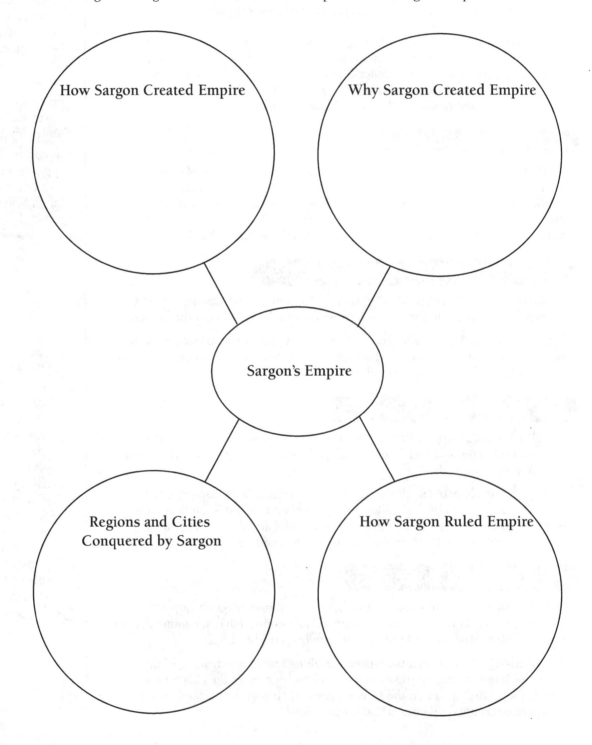

How Sargon Created Empire

Why Sargon Created Empire

Sargon's Empire

Regions and Cities
Conquered by Sargon

How Sargon Ruled Empire

NAME _____ **DATE** _____

A. MULTIPLE CHOICE

Circle the letter of the best answer for each question.

1. Historians know that Sargon actually ruled as a king from
   a. copies of "The Legend of Sargon."
   b. the autobiography of his daughter.
   c. his royal inscriptions.
   d. letters found at Ebla.

2. When Sargon conquered a city, he had its walls torn down to
   a. use the blocks for new defenses.
   b. end the city's independence.
   c. build houses for his followers.
   d. provide training for his soldiers.

3. Conquering lands in Syria and Lebanon meant that Sargon no longer had to
   a. worry about invasion from the north.
   b. pray to the gods of those lands.
   c. depend on southern cities for soldiers.
   d. trade for valuable lumber and metal.

4. The cuneiform texts found at Ebla show that the people of the city
   a. were paid very little.
   b. depended heavily on the king.
   c. did not have to work hard.
   d. were all farmers.

5. We can tell that the kings of Ebla communicated with rulers in other cities because
   a. they had their scribes write letters to the ruler of Hamazi.
   b. Sargon's name appears in their letters.
   c. their letters have been found in other cities.
   d. they and the other kings were brothers.

B. SHORT ANSWER

Write one or two sentences to answer each question.

6. How can scholars tell that Sargon probably wasn't from a royal family?

_____

_____

7. Why did Sargon pray to foreign gods as well as to his own?

_____

_____

8. Why did Sargon and other Mesopotamian kings probably send their scribes to foreign courts?

_____

_____

C. ESSAY

Reread the letter written by Tira-il (page 63). Then write an essay on a separate sheet of paper explaining what Ibubu was trying to express by his repeated use of the term *brother*.

CHAPTER 9

THE CARE AND FEEDING OF ANCIE
GODS: PRIESTESSES AND PRIESTS
IN MESOPOTAMIA

 VOCABULARY

Nanna Sumerian name for moon god; also called Ashimbabbar and Sin

Nippur home city of Enlil; Mesopotamians honored Nippur as a holy city

 WRITING

- **Poem** Have students choose a person whom they admire and write a poem to that person in the style of Enheduanna's "Hymn to Inanna."

CHAPTER SUMMARY

Priests and priestesses, including Sargon's daughter Enheduanna, held some of the highest positions in Mesopotamian society. They were charged with taking care of the gods and with administering the temples and their vast estates. Priests and priestesses sang hymns of praise to them and determined their will through omens. The gods were believed to occupy their cult statues, which received the food and drink.

PERFORMANCE OBJECTIVES

- ▶ To understand Mesopotamian religious rituals
- ▶ To analyze the connection between religion and government

BUILDING BACKGROUND

Elicit from students common activities of American religious leaders: leading prayer services, counseling congregation members, running religious schools, and so on. Emphasize that these activities all involve consistent contact with the public. Explain that students will learn about the different approach to religion in ancient Mesopotamia.

WORKING WITH PRIMARY SOURCES

Have students read the excerpt from Enheduanna's "Adoration of Inanna" in *The World in Ancient Times Primary Sources and Reference Volume*. (Longer versions of the hymn and of Enheduanna's other works can be found online: one source is *www-etcsl.orient.ox.ac.uk/section4/tr4072.htm*.) Have students analyze how the priestess addresses the goddess.

GEOGRAPHY CONNECTION

Location   Have students identify Ur on the map on page 61 and use the map scale to estimate its distance from Agade. Discuss with students why Sargon would want someone from his own family in an important position in this faraway city.

READING COMPREHENSION QUESTIONS

1. What was the purpose of Enheduanna's chants to Nanna and other gods and goddesses? (*She sang praises to the gods and prayed to them on behalf of her family, hoping to gain their favor for her father, Sargon.*)
2. What other daily duties did priests and priestesses have? (*They had to bathe, dress, and feed the statues of the gods in the temples, in which the gods were supposed to live. Some had specialized duties such as purifying the temple and divining the will of the gods.*)
3. What special treatment could wealthy Mesopotamians get from the temples? (*They could have statues of themselves placed in the temple to remind the god to watch over them.*)
4. What connection did most citizens have with the gods of their city? (*On festival days and holy days, the priests carried the statues of the gods and*

goddesses through the streets. All people had the day off for these events. There were also days when the gods went "visiting," or when the statues were carried to neighboring cities. These occasions were celebrated with feasts and dancing, which were organized by the priests and priestesses.)

CRITICAL THINKING QUESTIONS

1. Why did priests and priestesses have to be educated people who could read and write? *(Priests and priestesses had to be able to consult records of past events to be able to divine the god's will. They had to be able to read and write hymns to the gods.)*

2. Why could the position of high priestess or priest be a political appointment as well as a religious appointment? *(Possible answer: The high priestess or priest was appointed by the king. This person was supposed to pray to the gods to gain favor for the king as well as to watch over the local residents.)*

SOCIAL SCIENCES

Civics   Distribute copies of the blackline master for Chapter 9 to have students compare and contrast the relationship between religion and government in Sargon's empire with the relationship in the United States.

READING AND LANGUAGE ARTS

Reading Nonfiction   The chapter is anchored by the story of Sargon's priestess daughter, Enheduanna. Have students locate places in the chapter where her name is mentioned (besides at the beginning and the end). Then ask them how she is used to introduce other topics.

Using Language   Point out the use of the hyphen in the word *temple-owned* (page 67). Have students identify the parts of speech in this compound: it is an adjective made up of a noun and a verb. Point out the need for a hyphen when combining two words to make an adjective. Have them collect and create examples of their own.

SUPPORTING LEARNING

English Language Learners   Invite students to read aloud the description of religious holidays (page 69) and then summarize the text in their own words.

Struggling Readers   Have students use the outline graphic organizer (see the reproducibles at the back of this guide) to distinguish general information about religious practices from the specifics of Enheduanna's story.

EXTENDING LEARNING

Enrichment   The chapter says that diviners were supposed to figure out the will of the gods from various signs. Attempts to understand the will of gods occurs in other ancient civilizations. Have small groups investigate Chinese oracle bones, the oracles of Greece and Egypt, and other forms of ancient divination, and compare and contrast them with divination in Mesopotamia.

Extension   Have partners create dialogues between Enheduanna and one of her assistants. Enheduanna can reveal how she feels about writing and signing her name to her hymns. The assistant could show support, skepticism, or jealousy for the talented, self-confident Enheduanna.

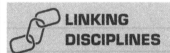

THEN and **NOW**

The first modern excavations of Nippur were carried out in the 1880s and 1890s. Since 1972, McGuire Gibson of the University of Chicago has overseen the Nippur dig, and many new artifacts have been recovered. This work is ongoing, and a report is published each year on new finds.

LINKING DISCIPLINES

Art Have students draw or make their own versions of the statues of the Mesopotamian gods. Each god should have a horned helmet, which was the mark of a god in Mesopotamia. Remind students to review what each god or goddess was responsible for (Chapter 5) so they can add ornamentation that expresses who the god is.

NAME   DATE

RELIGION AND GOVERNMENT: THEN AND NOW

Directions

For each statement about religion in the United States today, write a statement comparing or contrasting it with religion in the Mesopotamia of Sargon's time.

United States Today	Mesopotamia in Sargon's Time
Top officials of religions are appointed by religious groups.	
Religious organizations own land and buildings.	
Religious organizations hold festivals.	
Religious organizations invite all people to prayer services.	
Religious organizations hire local workers to maintain their buildings, run their offices, and do other jobs not done by the leaders.	

NAME   **DATE**

A. MULTIPLE CHOICE

Circle the letter of the best answer for each question.

1. Enheduanna's main job as priestess in the temple of Nanna was to
   a. be a servant to Nanna.
   b. cook sacred food for the workers.
   c. write hymns.
   d. teach at the temple school.

2. Mesopotamians believed that the spirit of each god lived
   a. in heaven.
   b. in the water.
   c. inside a cult statue.
   d. on a mountain.

3. Enheduanna became priestess in Ur because her father, Sargon, wanted to
   a. get her away from his court.
   b. control religion in this faraway city.
   c. ensure that she had a place to live.
   d. keep her from getting married.

4. Mesopotamian religion had practical effects on the people because
   a. all people could enter the temples.
   b. priestesses ran the government.
   c. many people worked for the temples.
   d. people got married in the temples.

5. Mesopotamians believed that bad luck was caused by
   a. a person's clumsiness.
   b. neglecting religious rituals.
   c. a person's actions in a former life.
   d. trying to change one's place in society.

B. SHORT ANSWER

Write one or two sentences to answer each question.

6. What would a priestess do to keep the gods happy?

7. Why was Nippur considered a holy city by Mesopotamians?

8. How would a Mesopotamian incorporate religion into daily life?

C. ESSAY

On a separate sheet of paper, write an essay comparing and contrasting the ways in which wealthy Mesopotamians practice religion and how common Mesopotamians would practice religion.

CHAPTER 10

LAYING DOWN THE LAW: HAMMURABI AND THE FIRST LAWMAKERS

PAGES 70–75

CAST OF CHARACTERS

Hammurabi (HAHM-oo-RAH-bee) king of Babylon who built an empire (ruled 1792–1750 BCE); author of collection of laws

Shulgi (SHOOL-gee) king of Third Dynasty of Ur (ruled 2094–2047 BCE); author of first collection of laws.

Ur-Nammu (ur-NAH-moo) king (2113–2096 BCE) of the Third Dynasty of Ur who built ziggurats

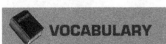

VOCABULARY

standardization establishing a standard rule for measuring weight, quantity, etc.

CHAPTER SUMMARY

Although Hammurabi is well known for his collection of laws, the first laws were written centuries earlier by a king of the third dynasty of Ur named Shulgi. Shulgi also made the roads safe to travel, standardized weights and measures, built ziggurats to the gods, and created a system to keep track of taxes and temple offerings. In the 18th century BCE Hammurabi built an empire almost as large as Sargon's but in his writings mostly emphasized the peaceful aspects of his reign, especially as a law-giver. His law collection is made up of about 280 laws that cover many aspects of Mesopotamian life. Crimes were punished largely with fines, though Hammurabi also introduced the idea of the punishment sometimes fitting the crime.

PERFORMANCE OBJECTIVES

▶ To analyze the law codes of Shulgi and Hammurabi
▶ To understand how the court system worked under Hammurabi

BUILDING BACKGROUND

Ask students what they know about the rules of your school. What do they regulate? What are the penalties for breaking the rules? Then elicit their knowledge of laws of your locality. Tell them that some of the groundwork for our present legal system can be found in four-thousand-year-old Mesopotamian law codes.

WORKING WITH PRIMARY SOURCES

Read aloud the quotations that refer to Shulgi and Hammurabi on pages 70, 72, 73, and 74. Tell students that these were either written by the kings themselves or that the kings had someone write them. Have students evaluate the usefulness of such primary sources to historians doing research on these personalities.

GEOGRAPHY CONNECTION

Location   Have students read the text to learn which cities were the capitals for Shulgi (Ur) and Hammurabi (Babylon). Then have them find these cities on the map on page 73. Tell them that both men ruled empires and not just a single city-state. Have students evaluate which city was better placed to be the capital of Mesopotamia and explain why.

READING COMPREHENSION QUESTIONS

1. What is Shulgi's reign known for? (*Shulgi's reign was peaceful. He built ziggurats, made the roads safe for travel, standardized weights and measures, kept track of taxes and payments, and wrote down a set of laws.*)
2. Why don't we know more about the reign of Hammurabi? (*The water level in the soil at Babylon has risen, soaking the clay records and the castle and turning them into mud.*)

3. Distribute copies of the blackline master for Chapter 10 so that students can study Hammurabi's laws.

CRITICAL THINKING QUESTIONS

1. Compare and contrast the law codes of Shulgi and Hammurabi. (*Shulgi listed numerous offenses and gave the fines that had to be paid for each one. Hammurabi also listed crimes and gave fines but added the idea that the punishment should match the crime. Thus, if a person blinded another person, the criminal should be blinded, too.*)

2. Have students read the epilogue to Hammurabi's laws in *The World in Ancient Times Primary Sources and Reference Volume* and restate in their own words the process by which someone who had been wronged could get justice.

SOCIAL SCIENCES

Civics   Have two teams debate this question: Can there be justice if laws are not written down? Students should research the reasons for having written laws and list some societies that have operated without them. Then the teams should present their arguments to the class.

READING AND LANGUAGE ARTS

Reading Nonfiction   Before they read the chapter, ask students why they think the authors opened a chapter about Hammurabi with information about Shulgi. After they have read the first three pages, have students explain what they gained by the authors' including the information.

Using Language   Introduce the suffixes *-ize* and *-ization* through the word *standardization* (page 71). Have students give examples of other words with those suffixes and arrive at a general definition.

SUPPORTING LEARNING

Struggling Readers   To compare and contrast the achievements of Shulgi and Hammurabi, have students use the Venn diagram graphic organizer (see the reproducibles at the back of this guide).

EXTENDING LEARNING

Enrichment   Download a translation of Hammurabi's laws from *www.fordham.edu/halsall/ancient/hamcode.html*, a website recommended in their book, and give appropriate sections to students. Have students analyze the laws according to the type of infraction addressed and the penalty involved. Students can share samples of interesting laws with the class.

Extension   Have students design a public relations campaign to get Shulgi the recognition he deserves for his set of laws.

LINKING DISCIPLINES

Art Have students illustrate one or more of Hammurabi's laws. Students can find some of the laws listed in *The World in Ancient Times Primary Sources and Reference Volume*. Students can write the law in ancient-looking script and add pictures as a border.

WRITING

Persuasion Have students write a persuasive paragraph about whether Hammurabi's "eye for an eye" concept is fair in all cases. Students should make up examples that support their point of view.

NAME   DATE

ANALYZING HAMMURABI'S LAWS

Directions
Read Hammurabi's laws and then answer the questions.

Law 3: If a man comes forward to give false testimony in a case but cannot bring evidence for his accusation [and] if that case involves a capital offense, that man shall be killed.
Law 4: If he comes forward to give false testimony for a case whose penalty is grain or silver, he shall be assessed the penalty for that case.
Law 22: If a man commits a robbery and is then seized, that man shall be killed.
Law 23: If the robber should not be seized, the man who has been robbed shall establish the extent of his lost property before the god; and the city and the governor in whose territory and district the robbery was committed shall replace his lost property to him.
Law 53: If a man neglects to reinforce the embankment of the irrigation canal of his field . . . and then a breach opens in its embankment and allows the water to carry away the common irrigated area, the man in whose embankment the breach opened shall replace the grain whose loss he caused.
Law 138: If a man intends to divorce his first-ranking wife who did not bear him children, he shall give her silver as much as was her bridewealth and restore to her the dowry that she brought from her father's house, and he shall divorce her.
Law 148: If a man marries a woman and later a skin disease seizes her and he decides to marry another woman, he will not divorce his wife whom the skin disease seized; she shall reside in quarters he constructs and he shall continue to support her as long as she lives.

1. What general areas do these laws address?

_____

_____

2. Why do you think that a person who has been robbed has to say what the lost property was "before the god" in order to get the property back (Law 23)?

_____

_____

3. How do Laws 138 and 148 protect both the man and the woman involved in a divorce?

_____

_____

A. MULTIPLE CHOICE

Circle the letter of the best answer for each question.

1. King Shulgi did all the following **except**
   a. build ziggurats.
   b. make roads safe for travelers.
   c. standardize weights and measures.
   d. open schools for all children.

2. Shulgi's laws included strict punishments in order to
   a. raise extra money for government.
   b. keep working people poor.
   c. discourage people from taking the law into their own hands.
   d. make sure that rich people would not break the laws.

3. Hammurabi freed people who sold their children or themselves into slavery by
   a. making slavery illegal.
   b. wiping out everyone's debts.
   c. paying off the money they owed.
   d. buying the slaves from their owners.

4. Hammurabi's law code sometimes forced the criminal to suffer
   a. the same fate as the victim.
   b. lifelong enslavement
   c. an easier fate than the victim.
   d. lifelong imprisonment.

5. An important part of Hammurabi's law code was that an accuser had to
   a. bring the accused person to court.
   b. pay a fee to the court.
   c. provide proof of the crime.
   d. pay for a lawyer.

B. SHORT ANSWER

Write one or two sentences to answer each question.

6. Why would a fine of 15 shekels of silver be considered a heavy fine by people living in Shulgi's time?

   _____

   _____

7. How did Hammurabi become an instant hero to the poor people in his empire?

   _____

   _____

8. What kinds of court cases did Hammurabi's laws cover?

   _____

   _____

C. ESSAY

On a separate sheet of paper, write an essay speculating on why Shulgi and Hammurabi decided to have written laws for their people. Did they do it because the size of their realms meant having written laws made governing easier? Did they believe that written laws were more fair? Or might there have been some other reason?

CHAPTER 11

ORDER IN THE COURT! THE JUSTICE SYSTEM IN MESOPOTAMIA

PAGES 76–79

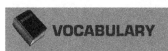

VOCABULARY

mina ancient unit of weight equal to approximately one pound

CAST OF CHARACTERS

Samsu-iluna (SAM-soo-ih-LOO-nah) son of Hammurabi; king (1749–1712 BCE) of Old Babylonian Empire

Ninshubur-tayar (nin-SHOO-bur-TIE-yar) 18th-century BCE farmer who adopted a son named Patiya

Patiya (pa-TEE-ya) young Mesopotamian man adopted by Ninshubur-tayar

Shamash-nasir (SHAH-mahsh-NAHT-seer) 18th-century BCE adopted son who went to court to claim his inheritance

CHAPTER SUMMARY

The Mesopotamian legal system was designed to find the truth in a legal case. Panels of judges considered evidence, interviewed witnesses, and asked the parties to a case to swear binding oaths. Written records were important to this process, including contracts that recorded the major transactions, and records of the court cases themselves, which have survived. People trusted the judges to be fair.

PERFORMANCE OBJECTIVES

▶ To understand the use of contracts and witnesses in Mesopotamia
▶ To summarize how decisions were made by Mesopotamian courts

BUILDING BACKGROUND

Read the title and subtitle aloud. Ask students what images the expression "order in the court" brings to mind for them. Elicit that a justice system handles many different kinds of cases, many of which involve disagreements between people rather than crimes.

WORKING WITH PRIMARY SOURCES

Have a volunteer read aloud the contract on page 77. Ask: How does the language of this contract differ from the language of the rest of the chapter? Elicit that the contract is drawn up in formal "legal" language that states facts and consequences clearly so that both sides understand exactly what the agreement is.

GEOGRAPHY CONNECTION

Interaction Have students look at the picture of the seal on page 77. Ask students what challenges would face a clerk if copies of Mesopotamian contracts had to be stored somewhere. Reinforce that the reason the Mesopotamians wrote on clay tablets was because that was the material they had to work with in their land.

READING COMPREHENSION QUESTIONS

1. What would happen to Ninshubur-tayar and Patiya if either of the men broke the adoption contract? (*Ninshubur-tayar would have to pay one third mina of silver and give Patiya his house and possessions. Patiya would have to one third mina of silver.*)
2. Why did some adoption agreements result in a court date? (*Sometimes biological children would be upset that an adoptive child was getting an inheritance and would try to get relief from the court.*)
3. What was the most important part in establishing the truth of a Mesopotamian contract? (*witnesses*)

CRITICAL THINKING QUESTIONS

1. Why did Ninshubur-tayar want to adopt Patiya? (*Ninshubur-tayar was getting old, and wanted someone to take care of him: farm his land, provide him with food, and pray for his soul after he died.*)
2. Why do people sign contracts when they make agreements like the ones described in the chapter? (*Possible answer: People want to make sure that the agreement will be carried out and that things will be set right if the agreement is broken.*)
3. Why would swearing in the presence of Shamash be a strong deterrent to lying in Mesopotamia? (*Shamash was thought to hate lying and might strike the liar dead on the spot.*)

SOCIAL SCIENCES

Economics   Have students investigate modern contracts. There are contracts of sale, rentals, employment, and so on. Have students find blank sample contracts online or in print sources. Small groups can compare the language of the contracts to each other and to the Mesopotamian contracts in the chapter.

READING AND LANGUAGE ARTS

Reading Nonfiction   The chapter opens with a story based in historical fact. Have students evaluate the effectiveness of starting the chapter this way. (They should recognize that it serves to arouse interest in the topic of the Mesopotamian justice system.) Ask: What topics introduced in the chapter opening appear later the chapter? Discuss alternative ways of opening the chapter.

Using Language   Have students compare the first and second paragraphs of the chapter to determine which sentences state facts and which are suppositions. Discuss how verbs such as *named, lived,* and *owned* indicate facts, while verb forms like *must have, seems to have* and the words *perhaps* and *probably* show the authors are imagining what happened.

SUPPORTING LEARNING

English Language Learners   Make sure students understand the references to "sticky fingers" (page 78) and "liar, liar, pants on fire" (page 79).

Struggling Readers   Have students use the cause and effect graphic organizer (see the reproducibles at the back of this guide) to show the effects of breaking laws described in the chapter.

EXTENDING LEARNING

Enrichment   Have a group of students compare the form of present-day contracts to that of Mesopotamian contracts.

Extension   Students can create a skit based on the court case described on page 79. Roles could include the judges, Shamash-nasir, his brother, and witnesses supporting Shamash-nasir. Given the outcome of the case described in the chapter, discuss students' opinions about whether justice was served.

WRITING

- **Contract** Have partners write a contract in which both agree to do something in return for something else. The wording should be precise so that there can be no argument over the terms. Have students trade contracts with others, who will try to find problems with the contracts.

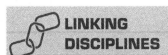

LINKING DISCIPLINES

Math Use the penalties cited in the Sticky Fingers, Beware! sidebar (page 78) to make up word problems for students: If someone steals an ox that is worth $100 from the palace, how much will he have to pay back? Have students make up their own word problems and trade them with partners.

WRITE A MESOPOTAMIAN CONTRACT

Directions

Imagine that you are living in Mesopotamia during the reign of Hammurabi. With a partner, use this form to create a contract in which you both agree to do something. It can be an adoption agreement, a sales agreement, a rental agreement, or an agreement of your choice. It should involve objects, activities, and forms of payment that existed in the time of Hammurabi. Make up seals for yourselves so you can sign the contract. Remember to get the seals of witnesses, too.

CONTRACT

_____ son/daughter of _____ and

_____ son/daughter of _____

Have agreed to the following:

_____ son/daughter of _____

will pay _____

to _____ son/daughter of _____
as the complete payment.

If either of them backs out of this agreement they will pay _____
to the palace.

Witnesses:

_____ son/daughter of _____

_____ son/daughter of _____

_____ son/daughter of _____

_____ scribe

(number)_____day of _____month in the year _____

_____   _____
Seal of First Party   Seal of Second Party

_____   _____
Seal of First Witness   Seal of Second Witness

A. MULTIPLE CHOICE

Circle the letter of the best answer for each question.

1. Why did Ninshubur-tayar draw up a contract describing his adoption agreement with Patiya?
   a. to protect Patiya from Ninshubur-tayar's children
   b. to ensure that Patiya would take care of him in his old age
   c. to ensure that Patiya could not take over Ninshubur-tayar's property
   d. to force Patiya to him for his property

2. In Mesopotamian courts, who did the talking for the people involved in the disagreement?
   a. scribes   c. the people themselves
   b. lawyers   d. the judges

3. Mesopotamian court cases were decided by
   a. a jury.   c. a group of judges.
   b. a priest and a priestess. d. friends of the two sides.

4. To be believed, witnesses had to declare their testimony in front of both the judges and
   a. their parents.   c. the god Shamash.
   b. the high priestess.   d. the god Enlil.

5. During Hammurabi's time, if a contract did not list witnesses, it
   a. was a good contract.   c. was complete.
   b. was not a good contract. d. would be approved by a judge.

B. SHORT ANSWER

Write a sentence or two to answer each question.

6. Why aren't Hammurabi's laws considered to be general rules?

   _____

   _____

7. For what kinds of situations did Mesopotamians use contracts?

   _____

   _____

8. Since Hammurabi's laws covered only certain court cases, what did judges have to do to decide many cases?

   _____

   _____

C. ESSAY

Reread the contract between Ninshubur-tayar and Patiya on page 77. Then write an essay on a separate sheet of paper stating your opinion of the fairness of the contract. Support your opinion by summarizing the duties of both men the penalties for breaking contract, and the benefits to both men.

Chapter 12   Farmers and Doctors, Barbers and Builders: Mesopotamian Workers, Slave and Free
Chapter 13   Ur-Utu's Story: The Mesopotamian Family
Chapter 14   Scribes, School, and Schoolboys: Education in Ancient Mesopotamia
Chapter 15   Lovers, Sisters, and Cooks: Scenes from a Mesopotamian Palace

UNIT OBJECTIVES

Unit 4 discusses everyday life in Mesopotamia at about the time of Hammurabi. It takes up the story of people who are not well documented in histories: workers, businesspeople, families, and children, and workers, as well as the everyday lives of kings and princesses. In this unit, your students will learn

▶ the activities of Mesopotamian workers and professionals.
▶ the relationships between family members.
▶ the training provided by Mesopotamian schools.
▶ the features of royal life.

PRIMARY SOURCES

Unit 4 includes excerpts from the following primary sources:

▶ Records from a queen's estate, 2400 BCE
▶ Laws of Eshnunna, 1900 BCE
▶ Laws of Hammurabi, 1755 BCE
▶ Dowry list, 17th century BCE
▶ Marriage contract, 17th century BCE
▶ Family letter, 19th–16th century BCE
▶ "Schooldays" story, 2000 BCE
▶ "The Disputation between Enkimansi and Girnishag" story, 2000 BCE
▶ Royal land gift contract, 1650 BCE
▶ Riddle
▶ Letter from Shibtu to Zimri-Lim, 18th century BCE
▶ Letter from Inib-sharri to Zimri-Lim, 18th century BCE
▶ Letter from Zimri-Lim to Inib-sharri, 18th century BCE
▶ Letter from Shimatum to Zimri-Lim, 18th century BCE
▶ Letter from Kirum to Zimri-Lim, 18th century BCE

Pictures of Mesopotamian artifacts from this era can also be analyzed as primary sources. Students can study these items to pull out details about Mesopotamian life:

▶ Relief sculpture of women spinning thread
▶ Temple weights, Mesopotamia
▶ Relief sculpture of Mesopotamian shopkeeper holding scales
▶ Plan of a Mesopotamian house from Ur
▶ Mesopotamian bed
▶ Mesopotamian board game
▶ Foundation of Ur-Utu's house

- ▶ Child's toys
- ▶ Student's school exercise tablet
- ▶ Painting of scribe
- ▶ Tablet showing plot of land
- ▶ Statue of woman, Mari
- ▶ Bronze statue of lion, Mari
- ▶ Palace wall painting, Mari

BIG IDEAS IN UNIT 4

Daily life, family, and **education** are the big ideas presented in Unit 4. The unit presents the activities of the Mesopotamian people as told by the thousands of tablets that have been found at certain sites as well as the excavations of numerous buildings from the time period.

Elicit from students their impressions of daily life in the modern world for both children and adults: going to work, going to school, running a household, communicating with others, and so on. Have students list these categories in their notebooks and use them to guide their reading of the unit.

GEOGRAPHY CONNECTION

Remind students that Mesopotamia was not a land that was rich in natural resources, and that valuable materials such as timber and metals had to be imported from elsewhere. Thus, building and writing materials—mud bricks and clay—were made from readily available resources that have survived through the millennia. This has provided archaeologists with a wealth of documents and building foundations to work with.

TIMELINE

Since this unit discusses lifestyle rather than events, chronology is not a major feature. The time period of the unit is approximately 2400 BCE to 1600 BCE, or from somewhat before Sargon's empire to somewhat after the time of Hammurabi.

UNIT PROJECTS

Artists' Conceptions

Have groups draw pictures or create dioramas of scenes from the unit. For example, they might depict the city street scene described in Chapter 12, the home of Inanna-Mansum and Ilsha-hegalli in Chapter 13, or a school scene from Chapter 14. Students can talk about their work and display it in class.

Role-Play

Ask a group of students to role-play the correspondence between Zimri-Lim and various people. They can make up responses to letters that do not appear in the text. Have students take on the roles of the correspondents and read their letters to the rest of the class.

Research Report

Small groups of students can investigate subjects of their choice to bring more information back to the rest of the class. Have students use the resources listed under Daily Life in the Further Reading section of their books. They can find pictures of cities on the Internet at sites listed on the Websites pages. Students' reports should have an oral as well as a written component. They should include visual aids for their oral reports.

ADDITIONAL ASSESSMENT

For Unit 4, divide the class into groups and have them all undertake the Research Report project so that you can assess their understanding of daily life in ancient Mesopotamia. Use the scoring rubric at the back of this guide to assess students' work, and have students rate their own work with the self-assessment rubric.

UNIVERSAL ACCESS

The following strategies are designed to cover a range of learning styles and reading, language, and skill levels. You may find that any of your students will benefit from various strategies presented.

Reading Strategies

▶ To facilitate reading, preview the artifacts in these chapters so that students will recognize the emphasis of this unit.
▶ Ask certain students to read aloud into a tape recorder. Play the tape back for them so they can hear themselves read aloud.
▶ Have partners read aloud to each other. When one partner has finished, the other can critique the reading so that the first partner can improve.

Writing Strategies

▶ Give students a list of categories with which to organize their notetaking in this unit. Possible categories include *Slaves, Workers, Professionals, Scribes, Marriage, Houses, Education,* and *Palace Life.*
▶ Have students summarize information in chapters by writing a first-person narrative about a day in the life of the people they meet in the chapters. They can use as their examples the Schooldays story on page 91 and the letter from Shibtu on page 95.

Listening and Speaking

▶ To spark students' interest, read aloud an excerpt from the chapter before having students read the chapter. Use an expressive tone of voice for best effect.
▶ Help teams of students role-play activities in the unit. Students should make basic masks and props to help their role-plays.

UNIT VOCABULARY LIST

The following words that appear in Unit 4 are important for your students'
understanding of the social studies content as well as for development of
literacy. Use these words for vocabulary study or to reinforce language arts skills
(e.g., synonyms, compound words, prefixes and suffixes, and related words).
The words are listed below in the order in which they appear in the chapters.

Chapter 12	Chapter 13	Chapter 14	Chapter 15
ration	arrangement	priestess	workshop
tanned	livestock	percentage	require
metalworker	basalt	claim	campaign
liter	dowry	calculate	fungus
aroma	exception	asphalt	water carrier
tavern	locust	benefit	diplomat
surplus	epidemic	exercise	cement
kiln	orchard	recited	allies
		self-employed	corridor
			elaborate
			fantastic
			pantry

FOR HOMEWORK

**STUDENT
STUDY GUIDE**

pages 33–34

 **VOCABULARY**

rations amount of food or supplies allotted to an individual or family

shekel a unit equal to about eight grams; used to measure silver and other valuable metals

luxury expensive and desirable, but not necessary for living

CAST OF CHARACTERS

Ningallam (nin-GAH-lahm) slave woman who raised pigs for queen's household in Lagash, 24th century BCE

CHAPTER SUMMARY

Many people, both slaves and free men and women, worked for the temples and palaces. They were involved in crafts such as textile production, animal husbandry, beer making, and metallurgy as well as in service to the priests and royal family. They were paid in rations or (for the highest ranking) in land that they could farm. Other people owned their own land or businesses, for example as bakers, innkeepers, barbers, physicians, and merchants.

PERFORMANCE OBJECTIVES

▶ To understand the range of economic activity in Mesopotamian cities
▶ To describe the daily activities of workers
▶ To understand the income of Mesopotamian workers

BUILDING BACKGROUND

Read the opening paragraph of the chapter aloud to students. Have them speculate on how the Mesopotamian texts—many of which were business records—would tell archaeologists about the lives of common people.

WORKING WITH PRIMARY SOURCES

Have students use the records of what a shekel of silver could buy from the Laws of Eshnunna to make inferences about the life of common workers. Help students relate the amounts of food to what they use in their own homes, and note food items that do not appear in the list. Help students realize that the list does not include finished articles, implying that the workers would have to make their own articles of clothing, bedding, and so on, or have them made by others.

GEOGRAPHY CONNECTION

Interaction As students read the chapter, help them recognize that, although trade was becoming more important to Mesopotamians, land was still the most important source of wealth. Have them note statements indicating that owning land and producing excess crops was the most prevalent form of survival as well as wealth-building.

READING COMPREHENSION QUESTIONS

1. What work did Mesopotamians do for the palaces and temples? (*They raised animals, wove cloth, made tools and weapons and jewelry, brewed beer, made furniture, carved statues and inscriptions, and tanned leather.*)
2. How would a typical Mesopotamian family get enough to eat? (*They would be paid for their work in grain and other foodstuffs. They would grow vegetables in a small garden and get fish from the river.*)
3. What kinds of professionals worked in Mesopotamian cities? (*physicians, veterinarians, builders, barbers, merchants*)

CRITICAL THINKING QUESTIONS

1. What would Ningallam and her children have done with the grain they received from the palace each month? (*They would probably grind it and make it into bread to eat. The text implies that they would not have gotten enough grain to trade for other articles.*)
2. Why were professionals able to thrive in Mesopotamian cities? (*Farmers were able to grow a surplus of crops, and some workers were paid more goods than they could use themselves. These people had either products or silver to trade for the objects professionals made or the services they provided.*)
3. Based on the information in the book, what might be the dangers of traveling to foreign places to trade? (*Trading agents might be attacked, robbed, and killed by criminals. They might face extremes of weather. If they traveled by boat, the boat might be sunk in a storm.*)

SOCIAL SCIENCES

Economies   Distribute copies of the blackline master for Chapter 12 so students can analyze the growing complexity of the Mesopotamian economy.

READING AND LANGUAGE ARTS

Reading Nonfiction   Have students identify the use of direct address in the description of the tour of the city. Ask them to evaluate the effectiveness of this approach for providing information. Invite students to describe a tour of the school for a new student using direct address.

Using Language   Challenge students to find the measurement equivalents given in the chapter (*gallon plastic milk jug* and *two squares from a chocolate bar*) on pages 80 and 82. Have them convert 42 liters to gallons and 8 grams to ounces to check the accuracy of the examples.

SUPPORTING LEARNING

English Language Learners   Students can work in pairs reading aloud the story of Ningallam (pages 80-81), defining unfamiliar words, and then retelling the story in their own words.

Struggling Readers   Have students make a three-column chart with the headings *Laborers*, *Professionals*, and *Merchants* to organize information about the lifestyle of people in Mesopotamian cities.

EXTENDING LEARNING

Enrichment   At the American Library Association website, students can learn how ancient documents are being preserved digitally: *www.ala.org/ala/booklist/speciallists/speciallistsandfeatures3/referenceonweb/claytabletsgo.htm.*

Extension   Students can work in small groups to design signs advertising stalls in the Southgate Mall mentioned at the end of the chapter. Signs should promote the services and products offered, as described in the chapter.

LINKING DISCIPLINES

Math Have partners use the figures given in the chapter to make up and solve riddles. For instance, they could use the "what a shekel of silver could buy" list to make riddles: If a person buys 2 pounds of wool, how much copper would she also be able to buy?

WRITING

Journal Have students imagine they live in a Mesopotamian city. Have them choose a job or profession, and write a journal entry about a day in their lives. They should include people they dealt with, trades they made, and other work they did.

THE MESOPOTAMIAN ECONOMY
IN THE TIME OF HAMMURABI

Directions

Many people make up an economy. Each person involved in an economy produces a service or a product. Each person also consumes services and products. In Mesopotamian cities, two dominant elements in the economy were the palace and the temples. The palace and the main temple each employed hundreds of workers. They would pay those workers in barley, wool, and oil, and then the workers would use their pay either to live or to trade for other things. Many other people were self-employed, owning small businesses, or owning land that they farmed.

Use the organizer to show the relationships between people in the economy of Mesopotamian cities. In each box, describe what product or service the person provided. Then, for each box, draw an arrow to another box and explain how that person was connected to somebody else in the economy.

Top Palace Official	Physician

Potter	Merchant

A. MULTIPLE CHOICE

Circle the letter of the best answer for each question.

1. The largest employers of workers in Mesopotamian cities were
   a. merchants and professionals.
   b. potters and farmers.
   c. palaces and temples.
   d. builders and brewers.

2. Mesopotamian workers who were paid in silver might get up to one shekel
   a. a day.
   b. a week.
   c. a month.
   d. a year.

3. Mesopotamian workers who received more barley than they needed for survival could
   a. ask for land instead.
   b. work fewer days.
   c. trade some barley for other goods.
   d. ask for animals instead.

4. One occupation that attracted women was
   a. physican.
   b. baker.
   c. trading agent.
   d. innkeeper.

5. Professionals who lived and worked in the city included
   a. physicians and barbers.
   b. farmers and miners.
   c. traders and metalworkers.
   d. innkeepers and builders..

B. SHORT ANSWER

Write one or two sentences to answer each question.

6. Why would pig farmers and metalworkers have worked in the countryside rather than near the palace?

_____

_____

7. How were the most important palace officials paid for their work?

_____

_____

8. How do we know so much about Mesopotamian daily life more than 4,000 years ago?

_____

_____

C. ESSAY

On a separate sheet of paper, write an essay in which you analyze the causes of the expansion of the economy of Mesopotamian cities at the time of Hammurabi.

UR-UTU'S STORY: THE MESOPOTAMIAN FAMILY

VOCABULARY

receipts records that prove ownership

dowry a woman's inheritance that she brings to her marriage

WRITING

○ **Description** Have students write a paragraph describing a typical Mesopotamian home, including the people who lived there.

THEN and NOW

The idea of a woman having a dowry when she gets married still exists today in cultures around the world, although it is not as important in societies where women and men both work and have their own incomes.

CHAPTER SUMMARY

Archaeological excavation of houses and the tablets they contain give us a glimpse of daily life in Mesopotamia. Marriages were arranged between two families, with the husband and wife (who was usually a teenager) both bringing material goods into the marriage. Contracts listed the terms of the marriage, including the possessions of each couple and the penalties for a divorce. Parents cherished their children. Those children who survived childhood illnesses tended to be taught at home—boys generally learned their father's business and girls learned to run the household from their mothers.

PERFORMANCE OBJECTIVES

▶ To understand Mesopotamian marriage arrangements
▶ To describe the layout of a typical Mesopotamian home
▶ To recognize details about Mesopotamian childhood

BUILDING BACKGROUND

Elicit from students what records their family might have that would tell about them and their ancestors. Ask them what an archaeologist might be able to tell from these documents. Then tell them they will read about the lives of people who lived 3,700 years ago reconstructed through such documents.

WORKING WITH PRIMARY SOURCES

Have students read the letter from a Babylonian son to his mother as well as the proverbs about family in *The World in Ancient Times Primary Sources and Reference Volume*. Have them discuss what effect the son's letter might have had on his mother, and why.

GEOGRAPHY CONNECTION

Location   Have students identify the location of Sippar on the map on pages 12–13. Have them give the location relative to other cities and physical features in the region.

READING COMPREHENSION QUESTIONS

1. Why was Ur-Utu so frantically searching through his records? (*Foreign tribes were attacking the city, and he had to flee, but he wanted to save records that proved his ownership of fields and other things that were the source of his wealth.*)
2. Ur-Utu's father married Ilsha-hegalli. What things did Ilsha-hegalli bring to the marriage in her dowry? (*She probably brought such things as a slave, a bed, chairs, a grindstone, cauldrons, chests, and garments.*)
3. After marriage, what was a Mesopotamian woman's relationship to her husband's family? To her own family? (*She became part of her husband's household, and lived amongst all his relatives. Yet she maintained a relationship*

with her own family, and was expected to help them if they had trouble of some sort.)

4. What did Mesopotamian parents do when their children became ill? *(They chanted, prayed, and put magical charms around the children's necks.)*

CRITICAL THINKING QUESTIONS

1. What conclusions can you draw about what concerned Ur-Utu by his actions during the attack on his city? *(Possible answer: He was very concerned about his wealth, since he seemed to be looking for the tablets that provided proof of what he owned.)*
2. Summarize the features of the Mesopotamian marriage contract. *(The marriage contract outlined what the wife would bring to the marriage in her dowry. It stated what would happen if either person broke the contract.)*
3. Distribute copies of the blackline master for Chapter 13 and have students summarize the relationships in a Mesopotamian family.

SOCIAL SCIENCES

Economies   Help students understand the economic status that a wife's dowry and her relationship with her own family gave her. Elicit that because the woman had her own wealth, and could get additional help from her own family, she wasn't completely dependent on her husband.

READING AND LANGUAGE ARTS

Reading Nonfiction   First have students locate the transition (page 87, third paragraph) between the two sections of the chapter—information about Ur-Utu's family and general information about Mesopotamian families. Discuss the effectiveness of using one family's experiences to teach about families in general.

Using Language   Have students read the title and subtitle of the chapter. Discuss the word *the* in the subtitle. Elicit that while *the* can indicate a particular person or thing, it can also be used to make a singular noun general, as in this case. Give an example, such as *the Siberian tiger lives in Asia,* and have students create their own examples of this use of the word *the.*

SUPPORTING LEARNING

Struggling Readers   Have students use the outline graphic organizer (see the reproducibles at the back of this guide) to identify the important general ideas of the chapter.

EXTENDING LEARNING

Enrichment   Have a group of interested students read a translation of Hammurabi's laws on marriage at the Internet Ancient History Sourcebook: *www.fordham.edu/halsall/ancient/hamcode.html.* They need to scroll down the numbered list of laws to items 133-145. After learning more about Hammurabi's marriage laws, they can report back to the class.

Extension   Invite one or more groups of students to make a checkerboard, copying the designs shown in the illustration on page 88. They can make a full-size board, using wood or heavy cardboard. Students can make checkers by cutting decorated circles from a heavy paper or cardboard (with adult supervision). Have them come up with rules for a game for two players that might be played using the board.

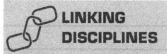

LINKING DISCIPLINES

Health Have students research modern safeguards against childhood diseases. For instance, the Centers for Disease Control publishes a schedule for childhood vaccinations against disease: *www.cdc.gov/ nip/recs/child-schedule.PDF.*

CAST OF CHARACTERS

Ur-Utu (ur-OO-too) wealthy Mesopotamian priest (17th century BCE) who kept an archive of his family business

Inanna-mansum (in-AHN-na-MAN-soon) priest and father of Ur-Utu

Ilsha-hegalli (IL-sha-hay-GAHL-lee) mother of Ur-Utu

Ra'imtum (ra-IM-tum) wife of Ur-Utu

A MESOPOTAMIAN FAMILY

Directions

The diagram shows the interrelationships between the parts of a Mesopotamian family. In each box, summarize the relationships of that person (or people) to the person in the box to which an arrow points.

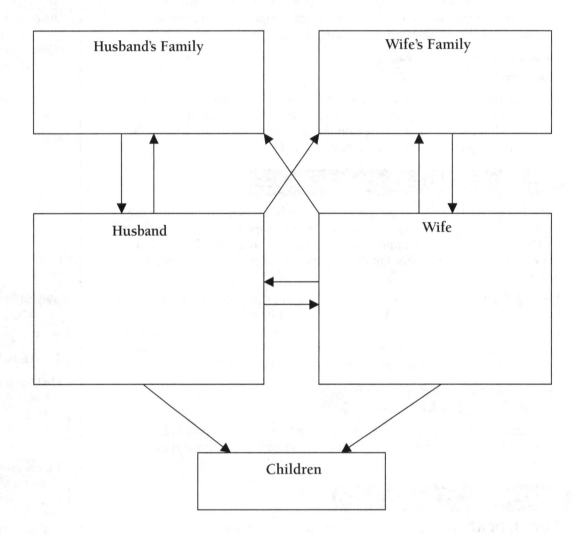

NAME   **DATE**

A. MULTIPLE CHOICE

Circle the letter of the best answer for each question.

1. Marriage in Mesopotamia was an arrangement between two
   a. families.   **c.** cities.
   b. individuals.   **d.** deities.

2. In order to arrange a marriage, the husband-to-be would have to do all of the following **except**
   a. become part of his wife's family.   **c.** prove he could support his wife.
   b. give his wife's father a gift.   **d.** make a marriage contract.

3. Mesopotamian homes were furnished with
   a. many tables and chairs.   **c.** paintings and vases.
   b. couches and desks.   **d.** rugs and cushions.

4. Mesopotamian women rarely held jobs outside the home because
   a. there were laws against that. **c.** they had large families to manage.
   b. they didn't need the money.   **d.** there were no jobs for women.

5. Mesopotamian parents tried to protect their children from disease through
   a. magic.   **c.** good hygiene.
   b. natural medicine.   **d.** healthy food.

B. SHORT ANSWER

Write one or two sentences to answer each question.

6. Who controlled a woman's dowry after she married? Why?

   _____

   _____

7. What relationship was a Mesopotamian woman expected to have with her own family after she was married?

   _____

   _____

8. How would Mesopotamian boys choose the career they would train for?

   _____

   _____

C. ESSAY

On a separate sheet of paper, write a character sketch of Ur-Utu based on the life that was reconstructed by archaeologists from his burned house. Include details about his family, his career, his wealth, and his wife.

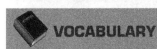 **VOCABULARY**

exercise assignment for students to complete

recited repeated aloud over and over

self-employed being in business for oneself

**CAST OF
CHARACTERS**

Pagirum (PAH-gee-rum) 17th-century BCE scribe who lived in Terqa

 WRITING

○ **Opinion** Have students put themselves in the place of Mesopotamian students. Have them write a paragraph stating their opinion of the education they are receiving. They should support their opinions with details from the chapter.

CHAPTER SUMMARY

Although most of the population was illiterate, scribes, priests, doctors, astronomers, and judges had to know how to read and write. They learned these skills as children at scribal school. The curriculum consisted largely of memorization and writing, and discipline was strict. Students also learned mathematics and they made copies of works of literature. Very few female scribes are known; the schools seem to have been almost exclusively for boys.

PERFORMANCE OBJECTIVES

▶ To understand what Mesopotamian boys studied
▶ To describe the Mesopotamian number system

BUILDING BACKGROUND

Elicit from students their impressions of the purpose of education: for example, to increase learning, to prepare for future career, to introduce arts and music. Ask what career young Mesopotamians would need schooling for (*scribe*) and what sort of training they would need (*language, reading, writing*).

WORKING WITH PRIMARY SOURCES

Have students read the excerpt from "Schooldays" in *The World in Ancient Times Primary Sources and Reference Volume.* This was a writing assignment in a scribal school from 2000 BCE. Have students summarize what the students studied and what discipline was like.

GEOGRAPHY CONNECTION

Interaction Being able to make calculations is extremely important to transactions such as land sales. Have students look at the plot on page 94, and have them recognize that figuring out the correct area of a piece of land would affect the purchase price. Bring in copies of local land surveys, such as the survey of the land your school is built on, and have students calculate the area of the plot.

READING COMPREHENSION QUESTIONS

1. For what careers did Mesopotamian education train young boys? (*scribe, doctor, judge, priest, astronomer*)
2. What kinds of families sent their children to school? (*wealthy families; parents who were scribes, kings, officials, and merchants*)
3. What were the rewards of an education? (*Boys who studied hard could become important and respected, and could become wealthy.*)

CRITICAL THINKING QUESTIONS

1. What did Mesopotamian boys learn in school besides the subjects they studied? *(Possible answer: They learned to follow rules and to respect their teachers and other people. If they did not, they were severely disciplined.)*

2. Why do you think there were no classes in history or science? *(Possible answer: History was learned in the tales and legends handed down from generation to generation, and in the stories that the students copied in learning how to write. Science, as we know it, did not exist as a subject at that time.)*

SOCIAL SCIENCES

Economy Have students relate the importance of well-trained scribes to the Mesopotamian economy. On the board, draw a two-column chart. In the left column, write the subjects that scribal students studied. Ask students what would happen if scribal students did not learn their subjects well (as in the excerpt from "The Disputation between Enkimansi and Girnishag" on page 94). Write the results in the right column.

READING AND LANGUAGE ARTS

Reading Nonfiction This chapter begins and ends with quotations and contains many more in between. Have students read aloud the quotations and assess their usefulness in conveying information and adding interest.

Using Language Have students define the words *scribe* and *professional* (page 92). Invite students to list and define these related words: *script, scribble, inscription, inscribe, proscribe;* and *profession, professor, profess.* Then ask students to use these words in original sentences.

SUPPORTING LEARNING

Struggling Readers Using information from the chapter, have students write a job description for a Mesopotamian scribe, listing his or her duties and the educational requirements for the job.

EXTENDING LEARNING

Enrichment Invite a group of students to illustrate the Mesopotamian riddle (page 94) and create their own riddles about school or other topics.

Extension Invite a group of students to find out more about Mesopotamian math and its connections to our system. Students can find out more, including how cuneiform numbers were written, at *http://it.stlawu.edu/~dmelvill/mesomath/.*

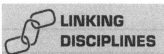

THEN and **NOW**

Have students compare the school schedule, types of exercises, and discipline techniques of your school with those of ancient Mesopotamian schools.

LINKING DISCIPLINES

Math Distribute copies of the blackline master for Chapter 14 so students can learn more about the Mesopotamian number system.

MESOPOTAMIAN CALCULATIONS

Directions

Read the information about the Mesopotamian number system, and then answer the questions.

For computation, the Mesopotamians used what is usually called a sexagesimal (base-60) system. They used combinations of two symbols bundled together for writing numbers up to 60. Here are the symbols:

$$\text{Y} = 1 \qquad \text{<} = 10$$

For writing numbers greater than 60, they just repeated the symbols in different columns, like we do. But where for us the values of each column increase by a factor of 10 (1s, 10s, 100s) as we move to the left, for Mesopotamians, the values of each column increased by a factor of 60 (1s, 60s, 3,600s). Here are some examples of Mesopotamian numbers, their place values translation, and the corresponding numbers in base 10.

Mesopotamian			Place Value Translation			Decimal Translation
3,600	60	1	3,600	60	1	
				1	15	75
				1	40	100
				16	43	1,003
			44	26	40	160,000

1. Translate the following Mesopotamian numbers into decimal numbers.

   a. _____

   b. _____

   c. _____

   d. _____

2. Write these decimal numbers using Mesopotamian numbers.

   a. 54 _____

   b. 147 _____

   c. 2,251 _____

   d. 56,258 _____

3. Write the ages of some of your friends and relatives using Mesopotamian numbers.

   _____

   _____

   _____

A. MULTIPLE CHOICE

Circle the letter of the best answer for each question.

1. Students in Mesopotamian schools were usually disciplined by
   a. being sent home.
   b. receiving a caning.
   c. having to copy sentences.
   d. having to sit in the corner.

2. Mesopotamian students studied all of these subjects **except**
   a. language.
   b. reading.
   c. science.
   d. writing.

3. Almost everything that scribal students studied involved work
   a. outdoors.
   b. on their tablets.
   c. on their own.
   d. in groups.

4. Students learned their lessons almost completely by
   a. listening to lectures.
   b. discussion.
   c. memorization.
   d. debate.

5. Scribal students had to learn the Sumerian language because it was
   a. the everyday language of the people.
   b. less difficult than Akkadian.
   c. the official language for contracts and letters.
   d. the only written language they had.

B. SHORT ANSWER

Write one or two sentences to answer each question.

6. What were the advantages of getting an education in Mesopotamia?

_____

_____

7. What do we know about female scribes in Mesopotamia?

_____

_____

8. What influences of the Mesopotamian number system still exist today?

_____

_____

C. ESSAY

Write an essay on a separate sheet of paper describing the experience of young Mesopotamians in scribal school.

CHAPTER 15

LOVERS, SISTERS, AND COOKS: SCENES FROM A MESOPOTAMIAN PALACE

PAGES 95–100

CAST OF CHARACTERS

Zimri-Lim (ZIM-ree-LIM) 18th-century BCE king of Mari

Shibtu (SHIB-too) wife of Zimri-Lim

Shimatum (SHIH-mah-toom) daughter of Zimri-Lim; wife of Haya-Sumu

Inib-sharri (IN-ib-SHAH-ree) daughter of Zimri-Lim

Kirum (KEY-room) daughter of Zimri-Lim; wife of Haya-Sumu

Haya-Sumu (HIE-ya-SOO-moo) 18th-century BCE Mesopotamian king who married daughters of Zimri-Lim

 VOCABULARY

wife Mesopotamian kings often had more than one wife, but other men could marry only one woman at a time

CHAPTER SUMMARY

The palace at Mari in Syria provides the best evidence for palace life in the time of Hammurabi. Its hundreds of opulent rooms and many courtyards were used not only by King Zimri-Lim and his family but by many servants and workers. Zimri-Lim's wife, Shibtu, and his daughters wrote to him often. Their letters, which were found in the palace, show that they helped the king: Shibtu ran the palace when Zimri-Lim was away, and his daughters, who were married to other kings, reported to Zimri-Lim on events in their lands (as well as complaining about their husbands).

PERFORMANCE OBJECTIVES

▶ To analyze documents to ascertain information about Mesopotamian life
▶ To describe how a palace was run
▶ To understand relations between kingdoms in Mesopotamia

BUILDING BACKGROUND

Remind students that the Mesopotamians kept meticulous records of their lives. Tell students that in the United States, the records of former presidents are commonly collected and stored on paper and in digital form in large libraries built specifically for that purpose. These records usually span a relatively short number of years. Have students think about what the records room for a Mesopotamian palace used for hundreds of years might be like.

WORKING WITH PRIMARY SOURCES

Have students analyze the texts of the Mari tablets presented in the chapter to draw conclusions about royal life at that time.

GEOGRAPHY CONNECTION

Location   Refer students to the map on pages 12–13 and have them find Mari. Ask them to give the location of Mari relative to other major cities and physical features. Have them estimate how long it would take an ambassador from various cities to travel to Mari.

READING COMPREHENSION QUESTIONS

1. Who were Zimri-Lim and Shibtu, and how do we know about them? *(They were an 18th-century BCE king of Mari and one of his wives. We know about them from their correspondence and other records found in the ruins of the Mari palace.)*
2. Why were so many of Zimri-Lim's daughters married to rulers of nearby lands? *(The marriages were used to cement alliances.)*
3. How large was the palace complex at Mari? *(The complex covered six acres, and it had more than 260 rooms.)*
4. Distribute copies of the blackline master for Chapter 15 and have students organize the information about the palace of Mari.

CRITICAL THINKING QUESTIONS

1. How did the marriage of a royal daughter to a nearby ruler help to cement an alliance? (*If the daughter and the ruler had children, the two kingdoms would be related by blood as well as by marriage. The daughter often sent back information about events in the nearby kingdom.*)

2. What were some of the risks of marrying a daughter to another ruler? (*The daughter might become unhappy or be treated poorly by the ruler. The daughter might not have any children by that ruler. This might endanger the alliance unless things were corrected.*)

SOCIAL SCIENCES

Civics   Have groups of students brainstorm the issues that kingdoms would have had to discuss in ancient Mesopotamia. Students should list general issues, such as common defense, trade, borders, coordination of religious festivals, and the like. Then they should include specific matters of importance in each category.

READING AND LANGUAGE ARTS

Reading Nonfiction   Call on students to read aloud from the letters quoted in this chapter. Encourage students to speak expressively and to use hand gestures where appropriate. Fit the passage to the reading abilities of each student.

Using Language   Have students investigate the definitions of these words and phrases found in the chapter *dehydration, fermentation, potted palm, scurrying,* and *seared,* and present the results of their research to the class.

SUPPORTING LEARNING

Struggling Readers   Have students look at the illustration of the palace on page 100 and read the caption. Then have them locate and list the palace workers mentioned in the chapter (pages 96 and 100) and discuss what each job included.

EXTENDING LEARNING

Enrichment   Students can find out more about Mari at *www.mnsu.edu/ emuseum/archaeology/sites/middle_east/mari.html* and at *http://atlastours.net/ syria/mari.html.* Have students prepare a report of their findings for the class, including pictures of the remains.

Extension   Have students prepare a skit based on a scene from the chapter, such as one portraying the rivalry between Shimatum and her sister Kirum (pages 97–98).

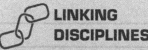

LINKING DISCIPLINES

Art Have students illustrate scenes from the chapter. Possible scenes could be Inib-sharri being treated insultingly by her husband or the arrival of the ambassador at the palace of Mari.

WRITING

Response to Literature Have students reread the letter from Inib-sharri to Zimri-Lim on page 97. Then have them write a paragraph explaining why Inib-sharri would have felt that her treatment by her husband was insulting.

RUNNING THE PALACE OF ZIMRI-LIM

Directions

Complete the chart with details from Chapter 15 to show what Zimri-Lim and Shibtu had to manage in their palace at Mari.

Category	What Had to Be Done
Health	
Royal Household	
Alliances	
Family Matters	
Official Visits by Ambassadors	
Royal Feasts	

A. MULTIPLE CHOICE

Circle the letter of the best answer for each question.

1. Zimri-Lim was an 18th-century BCE king of
   a. Mari.
   b. Sumeria.
   c. Babylon.
   d. Akkadia.

2. When Zimri-Lim was away at war, the palace was run by the king's
   a. chief minister.
   b. son.
   c. wife Shibtu.
   d. daughters.

3. To cement friendships with nearby kingdoms, Zimri-Lim
   a. sent his wife as an ambassador.
   b. married his daughters to other kings.
   c. paid tribute to other kings.
   d. sent his son as an ambassador.

4. Mesopotamian kings might take several wives to ensure that they would have
   a. help in the palace.
   b. better cooks.
   c. peace amongst the wives.
   d. heirs to follow them.

5. We know so much about Zimri-Lim because of the
   a. 20,000 tablets found at Mari.
   b. legends that have been handed down.
   c. writings of later historians.
   d. paintings on the wall of the palace.

B. SHORT ANSWER

Write one or two sentences to answer each question.

6. What unfortunate fate might befall a king's daughter who married a ruler of a neighboring kingdom?

   _____

   _____

7. How was Zimri-Lim kept informed of politics in neighboring lands and within his kingdom?

   _____

   _____

8. Describe the size of the palace at Mari.

   _____

   _____

C. ESSAY

On a separate sheet of paper, write an essay summarizing the ways in which Zimri-Lim dealt with nearby kingdoms.

Chapter 16	The Surprise Ending of the Babylonian Empire: Hittite Victories and Indo-European Languages
Chapter 17	Brides and Brother Kings: Diplomacy and the Great Powers

UNIT OBJECTIVES

Unit 5 discusses the rise of competing empires in the Near East, empires that eventually found a way to coexist for the benefit of all. The events of this time echo down to the present in the form of the Indo-European language of families and the discovery of how to purify iron ore. In this unit, your students will learn

▶ how Hittite conquests changed the power relationships in the Near East.
▶ where Indo-European languages originated and how they spread.
▶ how cooperation between Near East empires brought a prosperous International Age to the region.
▶ how the International Age came to a sudden, shocking end at the hands of the mysterious Sea Peoples.

PRIMARY SOURCES

Unit 5 includes excerpts from the following primary sources:

▶ Babylonian Chronicle, 1st millennium BCE
▶ Telipinu, Proclamation, 16th century BCE
▶ Hattusili, Annals of Hattusili, 17th century BCE
▶ Tushratta, Letter to wife of Amenhotep III, 14th century BCE
▶ Burra-buriyash, Letter to Amenhotep III, 14th century BCE
▶ King of Carchemish, Letter to King of Ugarit, 12th century BCE
▶ Ammurapi, Letter to King of Alashiya, 12th century BCE

Pictures of Near Eastern artifacts from this time period can also be analyzed as primary sources. Students can study these items to learn more about life in the International Age:

▶ Foundations of temple, Hattusa
▶ Bronze rein ring, Anatolia
▶ Bust of young Kassite man
▶ Cuneiform letter from Mittani's King Tushratta to Egypt's Queen Tiy
▶ Wall painting in Amenhotep III's palace, Egypt
▶ Statue of Egyptian god Bes
▶ Statue of Egyptian princess
▶ Gold bowl, Ugarit
▶ Roaring lion gateposts, Hattusa

BIG IDEAS IN UNIT 5

Conflict, cultural diffusion, and **cooperation** are the big ideas presented in Unit 5. The unit details the conflicts between peoples in the Near East as the great empires of the time fought for control of the land. These empires ended up sharing the region and trading with each other, rather than conquering each other. But the longest-lasting development from this time was the spread of Indo-European languages from near the Caspian Sea throughout the Near East, westward through Europe, and eastward to India.

GEOGRAPHY CONNECTION

This is the first unit that discusses the ancient Near East in a wider context. Have students look at the map on page 104 to show how the Near East was a crossroads of three continents—Asia, Africa, and Europe. Discuss how ideas as well as trade goods that originated in the Near East flowed outward and affected people in other regions as well.

TIMELINE

1900 BCE	Amorite dynasty founded; Old Babylonian period begins
1792–1750 BCE	Hammurabi creates Old Babylonian Empire
1775–1761 BCE	Zimri-Lim of Mari, Syria reigns
1749–1712 BCE	Samsu-iluna of Babylon reigns
1650 BCE	Foreign invaders destroy Sippar
1625–1595 BCE	Samsu-ditana of Babylon reigns
1595 BCE	Mursili of Hatti attacks Babylon; Old Babylonian Empire ends
1595–1500 BCE	Near East in turmoil
1500 BCE	Kassites in power in Babylonia; kingdom of Mittani begins; Hittite Empire grows
1387-1350 BCE	Amenhotep III reigns in Egypt; height of International Age; diplomatic marriages between Great Kings of Egypt, Babylonia, Mittani, and Hatti
1185 BCE	Invaders destroy Canaanite towns; Hittite capital is destroyed; Hittite Empire collapses
1176 BCE	Sea Peoples attack Egypt; International Age ends

UNIT PROJECTS

Dramatic Reading

Have groups of students prepare dramatic readings of scenes in this unit. One possibility is the attack on Ugarit by the unknown invaders. Another might be the letter from Tushratta to Amenhotep III found in *The World in Ancient Times Primary Sources and Reference Volume*.

Empire Building

The conflicts between empires in the Near East of this period are discussed in the *Ancient Egyptian World* volume of *The World in Ancient Times*. Students can use this resource as well as the resources listed on the Further Reading pages in their books to find out more about this conflict. Students could create historical maps of the region, showing the growth of the four mainland empires at different times. They can mark battle sites and other important sites, as well.

Research Report

Have a group of students find out what they can about the Sea Peoples and wandering invaders who destroyed the Hittite Empire, threatened Egypt, and may have caused the destruction of Mittani and Alashiya, too. Students can make a chart displaying the theories about these peoples: where they came from, what drove them to invade other lands, and where they went.

ADDITIONAL ASSESSMENT

For Unit 5, divide the class into groups and have them all undertake the Empire Building project so you can assess their understanding of the relationships between the Near Eastern empires of this time. Use the scoring rubric at the back of this guide to assess students' work, and have students rate their own work with the self-assessment rubric.

UNIVERSAL ACCESS

The following strategies are designed to cover a range of learning styles and reading, language, and skill levels. You may find that any of your students will benefit from various strategies presented.

Reading Strategies

▶ Have students read passages one-on-one with you to check their reading skills and comprehension.
▶ Have one student read a section of a chapter aloud to a partner, while the partner takes notes. Students should alternate roles.

Writing Strategies

▶ Have students imagine themselves as young assistants to some of the rulers named in this unit. They should write journal entries describing a day in their life.
▶ Have students use the sequence diagram (see reproducibles at the back of this guide) to place the events of this unit in order.

Listening and Speaking Strategies

▶ Have students read aloud excerpts from other Amarna letters. Students can present dramatic readings of the letters to show how the Near Eastern empires of the time worked together.
▶ Have partners write a dialogue between an interviewer and one of the personalities in this unit. Partners can present their dialogues to the class.

UNIT VOCABULARY LIST

The following words that appear in Unit 5 are important for your students'
understanding of the social studies content as well as for development of
literacy. Use these words for vocabulary study or to reinforce language arts skills
(e.g., synonyms, compound words, prefixes and suffixes, and related words).
The words are listed below in the order in which they appear in the chapters.

Chapter 16	Chapter 17
descendant	washbasin
demolish	union
murky	impurity
storm	lapis lazuli
assassin	ambassador
merge	pharaoh
advantage	refugee
smug	decline
wanna-be	dowry
	doting

FOR HOMEWORK

**STUDENT
STUDY GUIDE**

pages 41–42

VOCABULARY

language family group
of languages that have a
common ancestor

CAST OF CHARACTERS

Samsu-ditana (SAM-soo-dee-TAH-nah) last king of Old Babylonian Empire; ruler when Hittites raided Babylon

Mursili (MUHR-see-lee) Hittite king who raided Babylon in 1595 BCE

Sargon [SAR-gon] 24th-century BCE Mesopotamian warrior-king whose legendary exploits were retold through the ages

CHAPTER SUMMARY

The kingdom founded by Hammurabi was brought to end when the Hittites, led by Mursili I, conquered Babylon in 1595 BCE. The Hittites were from Anatolia (modern Turkey), and they later became a major power in the Near East. The Hittite language is the earliest Indo-European language to have been written down. Indo-European languages spread right across Europe, and into Persia and North India, as people speaking these languages migrated, probably from a region near the Caspian Sea, starting around 2500 BCE. English, Spanish, French, and most other European languages, are Indo-European. Some Hittite words are similar to their equivalents in these modern languages.

PERFORMANCE OBJECTIVES

► To describe the end of the Babylonian Empire
► To understand the similarities between the Indo-European languages

BUILDING BACKGROUND

Ask students to identify words in English that are similar in spelling or pronunciation to words in other languages. Students should be able to identify such words from other European languages. Tell them that the similarities are the result of these languages being related to each other, and that the earliest related language to be written down was Hittite.

WORKING WITH PRIMARY SOURCES

Have a volunteer read aloud the quote from the Babylonian Chronicle on page 101. Have students recall how archaeologists and historians attempt to determine dates of ancient texts and artifacts. (*compare with other sources, match styles with other artifacts whose dates are known*)

GEOGRAPHY CONNECTION

Place   Have students look at the map on pages 12-13 and locate the Hittites' homeland. Have them determine the distance from there to Babylon, and note any physical features (mountains) between the two states. Then have them draw conclusions about why the Hittites' conquest of Babylon was such as surprise.

READING COMPREHENSION QUESTIONS

1. Why was the Hittite conquest of Babylon surprising? (*At that time, Hatti wasn't a great power. It was a small kingdom in Anatolia.*)
2. What happened to the conquered Babylonians? (*The Hittites destroyed their city, stole their gold and their gods, killed many inhabitants, and took others with them into slavery.*)
3. Why are the Hittites important to speakers of many modern languages? (*Theirs was the first Indo-European language to be written down.*)
4. Distribute copies of the blackline master for Chapter 16 and have students compare the Indo-European languages.

CRITICAL THINKING QUESTIONS

1. Draw conclusions as to why the Hittites conquered and then left Babylon. (*Possible answers: thirst for conquest, desire for wealth, desire for glory*)
2. Why aren't the languages of the Indo-European group even more closely related to each other? (*The original language spread to many regions and acquired new words and ways of pronunciation. When people began writing down their languages, including Hittite, they were different from the original Indo-European language, which was never written down.*)

SOCIAL SCIENCES

Science, Technology, and Society   Have students make a list of words that describe modern technology, starting with the words listed on page 106. Have them use these words to draw conclusions about how languages change, and how different conditions from region to region and time to time cause different changes in language.

READING AND LANGUAGE ARTS

Reading Nonfiction   Have students look at the map on page 104 and point out the origin of the arrows (Anatolia) and the reason these languages are called Indo-European. The map is dated 2500–1000 BCE. Ask students if they think the languages in this "family" are still growing and changing. Have them give examples of categories of words used today that were unknown to people in 1000 BCE.

Using Language   Point out the statement on page 101: *Something terrible must have happened. But what?* Introduce the terms *foreshadowing* and *cliffhanger* and talk about how their use heightens reader interest.

SUPPORTING LEARNING

English Language Learners   Have students meet in small groups to discuss similarities among words in the chart on page 105. If feasible they can add words to the lists. Then have students use the English words in sentences.

Struggling Readers   Have students complete a main idea map (see reproducibles at the back of this guide) for each section of the chapter: Hittite victories and Indo-European languages.

EXTENDING LEARNING

Enrichment   Have a group of students investigate the excavation of the city of Hattusha at *www.hattuscha.de/eng/eng.html*, recommended on the Websites page of their book. The group can prepare a report on the excavations carried out by the German Institute of Archaeology.

Extension   Invite students to expand the Indo-European "cousins" chart on page 105. Students can copy it on a large sheet of paper, illustrate it, and find additional words at *www.colfa.utsa.edu/drinka/pie/pie.html*.

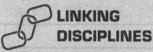

LINKING DISCIPLINES

Science Have groups learn more about linguistics and the study of similarities between languages. Have students find out how linguists make connections between languages (spelling, pronunciation, grammar, sentence structure) and report back to the class.

WRITING

Sentences Have students make up a list of archaic words that are not in common usage anymore. They can include words that they have heard from their older relatives, or examples from the dictionary. Have students write sentences using these words, trade them with partners, and then try to define what each word means.

INDO-EUROPEAN LANGUAGES

Directions

With a partner, use a dictionary or online resources to find words in other languages that are similar in spelling, pronunciation, and meaning to the English words in the chart. Find at least three examples for each English word. In the boxes, spell out the related word and tell the language it is from.

English Word	Language 1	Language 2	Language 3
mother			
father			
one, two, three			
bronze			
tree			
good			
drink			

A. MULTIPLE CHOICE

Circle the letter of the best answer for each question.

1. The kingdom of Babylon was destroyed in 1595 BCE by the
   a. Sumerians.
   b. Hittites.
   c. Kassites.
   d. Akkadians.

2. The conquerors of Babylon did all of the following **except**
   a. take the city's gold and silver.
   b. enslave the city's people.
   c. rule the city after its defeat.
   d. take the city's god statues.

3. By 1400 BCE, Mesopotamia had regained its strength under the rule of
   a. Mursili.
   b. Hattusili.
   c. Kassite kings.
   d. Farsi kings.

4. The origins of the Indo-European family of languages might be in the area of
   a. southern Mesopotamia.
   b. Persia.
   c. Egypt.
   d. the Caspian Sea.

5. As the Indo-Europeans spread out, their languages changed because they were influenced by
   a. priests.
   b. local languages.
   c. teachers.
   d. scribes.

B. SHORT ANSWER

Write one or two sentences to answer each question.

6. What did the Hittites do after they destroyed Babylon?

7. What weakened the Hittite state for almost two hundred years after the reign of Mursili I?

8. How did the fortunes of the Mesopotamians change under the rule of the Kassites?

C. ESSAY

Write an essay on a separate sheet of paper explaining why languages are constantly changing. Use examples of words in modern English.

FOR HOMEWORK

**STUDENT
STUDY GUIDE**

pages 43–44

CAST OF CHARACTERS

Amenhotep III (ah-men-HOE-tep) Egyptian king (1387–1350 BCE) who married the Mittani princess Tadu-Heba

Tadu-Heba (TAH-doo-HAY-bah) 14th century BCE princess of Mittani, daughter of Tushratta, wife of Amenhotep III

Tushratta (toosh-RAH-tah) 14th-century BCE king of Mittani; father of Tadu-Heba

Ammurapi (ah-moo-RAH-pee) last king of Ugarit (12th century BCE), an ancient city within the Hittite Empire

 **VOCABULARY**

diplomacy relations between foreign countries

ramparts defensive walls

CHAPTER SUMMARY

The period from around 1400 to 1200 has been called an "International Age" when the kings of the great powers of Egypt, Hatti (Turkey), Mittani (Syria), Babylonia and Alashiya (Cyprus) enjoyed close relationships through the exchange of letters and messengers (diplomacy), luxury trade, and intermarriage. This had come to an end by 1100 BCE when the major powers went into decline, in part as a result of attacks by groups that the Egyptians called the Sea Peoples.

PERFORMANCE OBJECTIVES

► To analyze the relations between empires and powerful kingdoms during the International Age
► To understand what ended the International Age

BUILDING BACKGROUND

Remind students of why Mesopotamian kings married their daughters to nearby kings—to cement alliances. Explain that during the 14th century BCE, kings sent their daughters much farther away, to empires whose cultures and languages were very different from their own.

WORKING WITH PRIMARY SOURCES

Have volunteers read aloud the letters between rulers described in the chapter and the Amarna letter in *The World in Ancient Times Primary Sources and Reference Volume*. Help students analyze the tone of each letter, and what they can tell about the relationship between the writer and the recipient.

GEOGRAPHY CONNECTION

Regions Have students look at the map on page 111, and then leaf through preceding chapters to note other maps. Elicit that most of the maps to this point have concentrated on Mesopotamia and Syria. Discuss how this map is different.

READING COMPREHENSION QUESTIONS

1. Who was Princess Tadu-Heba getting married to? (*Amenhotep III of Egypt*)
2. Name the five great powers of the Near East at this time. (*Egypt, Babylon, Mittani, Hatti, Alashiya*)
3. Why did Hatti and Egypt both fight against Mittani in the 15th century BCE? Why did they stop fighting? (*Mittani wanted more land and a port on the Mediterranean, which conflicted with the aims of Egypt and Hatti. Eventually, the kingdoms' borders became more settled and the powers decided to cooperate and trade rather than fight.*)
4. How did the International Age come to an end? (*Hatti, Alashiya, and Egypt were attacked in the early years of the 12th century BCE by invaders that may have been related to the Sea Peoples. Babylonia and Egypt were weakened, and Mittani, Hatti, and Alashiya disappeared. Trade shriveled to almost nothing.*)

CRITICAL THINKING QUESTIONS

1. What characteristics did the five great powers share? (*Four of them—Hatti, Mittani, Babylon, and Egypt—controlled large land areas and had powerful armies. They all had valuable resources that they could trade with each other. They all used Akkadian in their diplomatic dealings with each other.*)

2. Why weren't the five Great Kings able to work together to defend their lands from the Sea Peoples and other invaders? (*The distances in the region are so great, and travel was so slow at the time, that rulers could not move their armies quickly from one place to another. Also, the relationships between the powers were sometimes tense. They put their own interests first in times of crisis.*)

3. Why do you think the king of Babylon (in the Why Don't You Write Me? sidebar) had never visited Egypt and didn't know how far away it was? (*Kings could not leave their countries for the many months it would take to visit a foreign land because their thrones might be usurped in their absence. They had to depend on their ambassadors and messengers to tell them about the other lands.*)

SOCIAL SCIENCES

Economics   The chapter says that Alashiya got into the Great King club because it had large amounts of copper, an important ingredient in bronze, with which all of the kingdoms made their weapons and tools. Discuss the concept of economic power. Draw comparisons between this ancient situation and modern equivalents, such as small countries that have large reserves of oil.

READING AND LANGUAGE ARTS

Reading Nonfiction   Have students preview the chapter by looking at the title, pictures, graphic aids, and sidebars. Help them formulate questions that they expect will be answered by the chapter.

Using Language   Point out the simile in the first sentence of paragraph 3 on page 112: *enemy ships waiting to attack like hawks eyeing their prey.* Ask what feelings this simile evokes. Now have students consider the metaphor in the next paragraph, *hopes . . . dashed on the rocks of disappointment.* Ask students to create their own similes and metaphors.

SUPPORTING LEARNING

English Language Learners   Point out the colloquialisms—expressions used in casual conversation—on pages 107, 109, 110, and 113: *dress the part, Great King club, empire-building bug, glory days,* and *name of the game.* Have partners use context clues to explain the meaning of these expressions.

Struggling Readers   Students can use the sequence of events graphic organizer (see reproducibles at the back of this guide) to better understand the chronology of the chapter. They should refer to the Timeline on page 113 but use their own words in completing the chart.

EXTENDING LEARNING

Enrichment   Students can find out more about the invaders of Ugarit, called the Sea Peoples by the Egyptians, at *www.touregypt.net/featurestories/seapeople.htm.*

Extension   Students can use the map scale on page 111 to determine distances between places mentioned in the chapter.

WRITING

Journal Have students write a journal entry describing the entry of Princess Tadu-Heba into Thebes.

LINKING DISCIPLINES

Art Have students illustrate scenes from the chapter, such as Tadu-Heba arriving at Thebes or the attack on Ugarit.

THEN and NOW

Akkadian was the language of diplomacy for the five Great Kings. Through the years, different languages have been standard diplomatic languages because of their wide use or the influence of their native speakers. The most prevalent diplomatic language now is English because of the worldwide influence of the United States since World War II and of the British Empire before then.

THE FIVE POWERS OF THE INTERNATIONAL AGE

Directions

Use the map and information from your book to answer the questions.

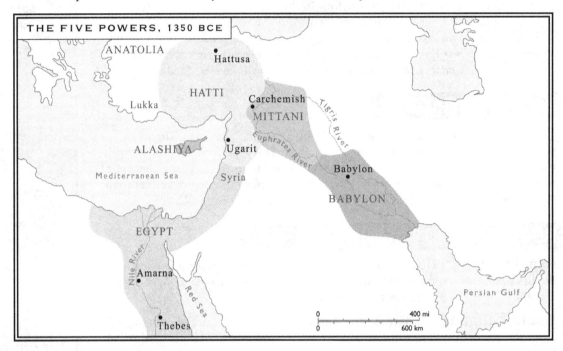

THE FIVE POWERS, 1350 BCE

1. During the International Age, trade flourished in the Near Eastern world. Using the information in Chapter 17 and previous chapters, label on the map the goods that each of these lands had to trade.

2. Chapter 17 says that the journey from Babylon to Amarna was more than 1,500 miles. Measure and draw a possible route of that length between the two cities.

3. Why wouldn't a traveler be able to take a more direct route between Babylon and Amarna?

_____

_____

NAME   **DATE**

A. MULTIPLE CHOICE

Circle the letter of the best answer for each question.

1. King Amenhotep III of Egypt was married to
   a. a goddess.
   b. wives from all over the Near East.
   c. a priestess.
   d. only one woman.

2. The rulers of Near Eastern kingdoms exchanged gifts and princesses in order to
   a. pay their debts.
   b. conquer new lands.
   c. have hostages from other lands.
   d. maintain peaceful relations.

3. The five "brother" kings of the Near East found that trade and cooperation between them were better than
   a. trading with other regions.
   b. building their own economies.
   c. trying to conquer each other.
   d. digging their own mines.

4. The diplomatic language used by the five Great Kings was
   a. Akkadian.
   b. Sumerian.
   c. Egyptian.
   d. Hittite.

5. The International Age in the Near East lasted until
   a. Egypt conquered the other kingdoms.
   b. the Hittites migrated to Europe.
   c. Mittani conquered Babylon.
   d. invaders attacked Egypt, Alashiya, and Hatti.

B. SHORT ANSWER

Write one or two sentences to answer each question.

6. How was Egypt different than the rest of the Near Eastern world?

_____

_____

7. Why were the Hittites, Mittani, and Egyptians often at war in the 15th century BCE?

_____

_____

8. Describe the situation in the Near East by 1100 BCE.

_____

_____

C. ESSAY

On a separate sheet of paper, write an essay describing how international relations were carried out in the Near East during the 14th century BCE.

UNIT OBJECTIVES

Unit 6 discusses the history of one of the peoples in the ancient Near East that
had the most lasting influence on world history: the Israelites. In this unit, your
students will learn about

► the origins of the Israelites and their early rulers.
► how the Israelites' beliefs set them apart from the other Near Eastern
peoples.
► the Israelites' laws and ideas of divine justice.

PRIMARY SOURCES

Unit 6 includes excerpts from the following primary sources:

► Azitawadda, royal inscription
► I Samuel, Hebrew Bible
► Book of Proverbs, Hebrew Bible
► Anonymous Egyptian, "The Instruction of Amen-em-opet"
► I Kings, Hebrew Bible
► Mesha, Moabite Stone
► Genesis, Hebrew Bible
► "Myth of Atrahasis," 17th century BCE
► II Kings, Hebrew Bible
► Exodus, Hebrew Bible
► Deuteronomy, Hebrew Bible
► Book of Psalms, Hebrew Bible

Pictures of Near Eastern artifacts in this unit can also be analyzed as primary
sources. Students can study these items to pull out details on the lives of the
Israelites:

► Painting of Samuel anointing David
► Relief sculpture of man with sling
► Clay coffin from excavation site in Israel
► Oil lamp
► Early Christian mosaic of Moses parting the Red Sea
► Statue of Canaanite god that might be Baal

BIG IDEAS IN UNIT 6

Movement, religion, and **law** are the big ideas presented in Unit 6. The unit begins with information about the Israelites' arrival and subsequent kingdoms in Canaan, in the Near East close to the Mediterranean Sea. It then discusses the religious beliefs of the Israelites and the laws of these people. One way to introduce these ideas is to discuss what students know about the Israelites (or Hebrews or Jews, as they were known later). Elicit stories from the Old Testament, such as the Exodus from Egypt, the Ten Commandments, and so on. Express the idea that, through the ages, the Israelites maintained a strong identity as a separate and united people because of their shared beliefs.

GEOGRAPHY CONNECTION

According to Biblical accounts, the Israelites were a people who originated near Ur in southern Mesopotamia. They believed that their patriarch, Abraham, was told by the Hebrew god, Yahweh, to leave his homeland and travel to Canaan. Abraham was supposed to have settled in the region of present-day Jerusalem. The Bible recounts that many Israelites later migrated to Egypt, and then many years after that, migrated back to Canaan, were they established the kingdom of Israel.

TIMELINE

1200 BCE	Israelites arrive in Levant
1020 BCE	Saul's reign begins
1000 BCE	David's reign begins
960 BCE	Solomon's reign begins
922 BCE	Israel divides into two kingdoms
722 BCE	Assyrians conquer Israel
598–597 BCE	Jehoiakin of Judah reigns
587 BCE	Judah conquered by Babylonia; Babylonian exile begins
539 BCE	Jews return to Jerusalem

UNIT PROJECTS

Dramatic Reading

Have a group of students prepare a dramatic reading of the Adam and Eve story in *The World in Ancient Times Primary Sources and Reference Volume* and present it to the class.

Famous Israelites

Since the Bible is the history of the Israelites, have students read excerpts from the Bible that tell about the personalities mentioned in the book. Excerpts from the Hebrew Bible can be found at the Internet Ancient History Sourcebook *www.fordham.edu/halsall/ancient/asbook.html,* which is included on the Websites page of the book. Students can use the information to compare and contrast rulers such as Saul, David, and Solomon.

ADDITIONAL ASSESSMENT

For Unit 6, divide the class into groups and have them all undertake the Famous Israelites project so you can assess their understanding of the history of the Israelites. Use the scoring rubric at the back of this guide to assess students' work, and have students rate their own work with the self-assessment rubric.

UNIVERSAL ACCESS

The following strategies are designed to cover a range of learning styles and reading, language, and skill levels. You may find that any of your students will benefit from various strategies presented.

Reading Strategies

▶ Have the class read the chapters aloud. Stop the reading from time to time and lead students in taking notes about the text.

▶ Have students read the chapters in small groups. When they are done, one group member should act as the Questioner and ask questions about the text. Other group members should answer with details from the chapter.

Writing Strategies

▶ Have students put themselves in the place of David, Adam or Eve, Noah, or other personalities in the unit. Have them write journal entries describing their feelings about the important events discussed in the chapters.

▶ Have students summarize the ten laws of Moses in their own words.

▶ The events in Chapter 18 are followed by the events in Chapter 20. Chapter 19 pauses to look at the Israelites' beliefs about God and about their origins. When students take notes on Chapters 18 and 20, have them begin each page with the approximate dates covered by each chapter. Note that the stories in Chapter 19 cannot be assigned dates.

Listening and Speaking Strategies

▶ Have small groups analyze the concepts and events that welded the Israelites into a unified people. Groups can use a round-table format, with each group member stating one concept or event and how it helped create unity.

▶ Have partners write questions for each other about the topics of the chapters. Each partner should take the role of one of the personalities in the chapter to answer the other partner's questions.

UNIT VOCABULARY LIST

The following words that appear in Unit 6 are important for your students' understanding of the social studies content as well as for development of literacy. Use these words for vocabulary study or to reinforce language arts skills (e.g., synonyms, compound words, prefixes and suffixes, and related words). The words are listed below in the order in which they appear in the chapters.

Chapter 18	**Chapter 19**	**Chapter 20**
editor	slithery	just
churn	floodwater	secretary
potential	burdensome	symbolize
anoint	retold	bulrush
flourish	famine	infest
border	identity	essential
credit		absolute
penned		conditional
covenant		expand
		monotheism

CAST OF CHARACTERS

Saul first king of Israel (11th century BCE) who often fought against the Philistines

David second king of Israel (around 1000 BCE) who united the Israelites and made Jerusalem the capital

Samuel 11th-century BCE Israelite religious leader who anointed Saul and David

Solomon (SOLL-uh-mun) son of David, ruler of Israel (10th century BCE) who built temple to Yahweh in Jerusalem

Omri (OHM-ree) king of Israel (885–874 BCE) who sent tribute to Assyria

Ruth Moabite woman; described in Hebrew Bible as Naomi's daughter-in-law and great-grandmother of David

Naomi Israelite woman described in Hebrew Bible as mother-in-law of Ruth and great-great-grandmother of David

CHAPTER SUMMARY

After the great powers collapsed, small kingdoms dominated the Levant (modern Jordan, Syria, Israel, Lebanon, and the Palestinian territories). These included Israel, which is better known than the others because of the stories in the Hebrew Bible. The Bible records a time of warfare between the Israelites, Canaanites, and Philistines, during which the Israelites chose to have a king. The first king, Saul, was followed by David, who was able to unify the land. His son, Solomon, traded with neighboring lands and built a temple to the Israelite god Yahweh, in Jerusalem. After Solomon's death the land split in two: Israel in the north and Judah in the south.

PERFORMANCE OBJECTIVES

▶ To analyze the origins of the ancient kingdom of Israel
▶ To recognize historical aspects of the Hebrew Bible
▶ To describe the accomplishments of the early Israelite kings

BUILDING BACKGROUND

Elicit students' knowledge of the story of David and Goliath, and then read aloud the excerpt from the Biblical account of their duel on page 117. Make sure students understand that David was a historical figure

WORKING WITH PRIMARY SOURCES

Have students read the excerpt about Saul and David in The *World in Ancient Times Primary Sources and Reference Volume*. Discuss the tradition in the Near East of success meaning that god (or, in other lands, the gods) was on your side.

GEOGRAPHY CONNECTION

Place Have students look at the map on page 115 and identify the physical features that made the Levant a good place for agriculture. (*availability of water from Sea of Galilee and Jordan River, adequate rainfall in many places, though that isn't shown on the map*)

READING COMPREHENSION QUESTIONS

1. What set the Israelites apart from the other peoples of the Levant? (*They thought it was important to write down their history. Their writings were collected later as the Hebrew Bible, or Christian Old Testament, which gives us a lot of evidence about their lives.*)
2. Why did the Israelites decide they needed a king? (*The 12 tribes would unite only when they were fighting other people, but repeated defeats caused them to seek a closer connection.*)
3. What were the accomplishments of King David? (*David killed the giant Goliath and later defeated the Philistines. He ruled over Canaanites, Hittites, and Philistines as well as Israelites, and established his capital at Jerusalem. He brought the Ark of the Covenant into Jerusalem.*)

4. What happened to Israel after Solomon's death? (*The country split in two, with the southern part changing its name to Judah and the northern part keeping the name Israel. The two countries coexisted for 200 years, sometimes friendly, sometimes at war.*)

5. Distribute copies of the blackline master for Chapter 18 to help students organize the information in the chapter.

CRITICAL THINKING QUESTIONS

1. What was the source of Israel's wealth? (*The land was good for agriculture, and it was a crossroads for traders.*)

2. How was Israel, in Solomon's time, similar to the Great Powers of previous centuries? (*Solomon traded with neighboring kings, and married foreign princesses; his reign was peaceful and prosperous.*)

SOCIAL SCIENCES

Civics   The chapter says that the Israelites didn't unite under a single king until repeated military defeats showed they needed a king. Ask students to explain why such a situation would make people decide to work more closely together. (*stronger military organization, easier to fight wars with one military force*) Elicit other reasons why different people in the Near East chose a single leader.

READING AND LANGUAGE ARTS

Reading Nonfiction   The chapter states that the Israelites differed from other peoples in that they wrote down their history in books. As students read the chapter, have them note evidence of this statement and draw conclusions about its importance.

Using Language   Have students define the word *testament* (sidebar, page 117) and the related words *testify, testimonial,* and *testimony.*

SUPPORTING LEARNING

English Language Learners   In a small group, have students read aloud the quotations from the Book of Proverbs and "The Instruction of Amen-em-opet" in the box on page 118. Define *proverb* and then point out the similes *flying like an eagle* and *wings like geese.* Discuss how the similes enhance the impact of the sayings. Encourage students to create their own proverbs about wealth and riches.

Struggling Readers   Have students create a sequence of events graphic organizer (see reproducibles at the back of this guide) to help them understand the historical content covered in the chapter.

EXTENDING LEARNING

Enrichment   Students can read more of the Book of Proverbs online at *www.mechon-mamre.org/e/et/et2801.htm.*

Extension   Students can create illustrations and captions for the stories in this chapter: Naomi and Ruth and David and Goliath.

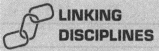

LINKING DISCIPLINES

Math The giant Goliath has been variously described as about 4 cubits tall to more than 6 cubits tall. Explain that a cubit was an ancient measure equal to the length of the forearm from the elbow to the tip of the middle finger (usually 18–20 inches). Have them compute the height range given for Goliath in feet and inches, and then use cubits to measure common classroom articles.

WRITING

Narrative Have students write about the duel between David and Goliath, giving a "blow-by-blow" account of the action.

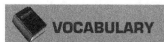

VOCABULARY

Levant the lands of modern Israel, Jordan, Lebanon, and the Palestinian territories

anoint to make holy through religious ritual, often involving holy oil

NAME   **DATE**

EARLY ISRAELITE KINGS

Directions

Use the chart to evaluate the leadership of the early Israelites. In the second column, tell what happened during each time period. In the third column, tell what you think are the positive and negative aspects of the ruler.

Leadership	Major Events	Evaluation
Various military rulers		
Saul		
David		
Solomon		

NAME   **DATE**

A. MULTIPLE CHOICE

Circle the letter of the best answer for each question.

1. The language that spread throughout the Near East during the dark ages was
   - **a.** Egyptian.
   - **b.** Akkadian.
   - **c.** Aramaic.
   - **d.** Israeli.

2. According to the Hebrew Bible, the Israelites arrived in the Levant around 1200 BCE after
   - **a.** defeating the Egyptian army.
   - **b.** escaping from slavery in Egypt.
   - **c.** crossing the Mediterranean Sea.
   - **d.** migrating from Babylon.

3. In order to claim their land, the Israelites had to battle
   - **a.** Kassites and Philistines.
   - **b.** Kassites and Canaanites.
   - **c.** Philistines and Assyrians.
   - **d.** Canaanites and Philistines.

4. In chronological order, the first three kings of Israel were
   - **a.** Saul, David, and Omri.
   - **b.** Azitawadda, Saul, and David.
   - **c.** Saul, David, and Solomon.
   - **d.** Omri, David, and Solomon.

5. After Solomon's death, the kingdom of Israel
   - **a.** was destroyed.
   - **b.** broke into two kingdoms.
   - **c.** became a large empire.
   - **d.** became part of the Egyptian empire.

B. SHORT ANSWER

Write one or two sentences to answer each question.

6. How was the Hebrew Bible created?

   _____

   _____

7. How did David become king of Israel?

   _____

   _____

8. What evidence do we have that Solomon's reign was prosperous for Israel?

   _____

   _____

C. ESSAY

Write an essay on a separate sheet of paper summarizing how the kingdom of Israel was created and developed under its first three kings.

CHAPTER 19

ONE GOD, MANY STORIES: THE BELIEFS OF THE ISRAELITES

PAGES 120–124

FOR HOMEWORK

STUDENT STUDY GUIDE

pages 47–48

CAST OF CHARACTERS

Adam man described in the Hebrew Bible as the first human being

Eve person described in the Hebrew Bible as the first woman

Noah man described in the Hebrew Bible as the good man who survived a great flood

Abraham man described in the Hebrew Bible as the patriarch of the Israelites

Isaac (EYE-zak) son of Abraham; described in the Hebrew Bible as the father of the Israelites

Ishmael (ISH-may-el) son of Abraham; described in the Hebrew Bible as the father of the Arabs

Jacob described in the Hebrew Bible as a great Israelite leader; son of Isaac; father of Joseph

Joseph grandson of Isaac, according to the Hebrew Bible; became powerful in Egypt

CHAPTER SUMMARY

The Israelite writers of the Bible believed in one god, Yahweh, unlike their polytheistic neighbors who worshiped many gods. The Bible records their religious beliefs, including the creation of the universe and of humans by Yahweh, and a great flood that he sent to punish humankind. Similarities with a flood story in Mesopotamia probably result from a common original tale, but the two stories reflect different religious beliefs.

PERFORMANCE OBJECTIVES

▶ To use primary source documents to understand the religion of the Israelites
▶ To compare and contrast religious traditions
▶ To understand the Israelites' beliefs about their origins

BUILDING BACKGROUND

Ask students how the ancient Near Eastern religions they have been studying differ from the religions that most people in the United States follow. (*Ancient Near East religions worshiped many gods; western religions worship one god.*) Explain that this chapter takes them back to the beginning of monotheistic religion.

WORKING WITH PRIMARY SOURCES

Have students make direct comparison and contrasts of the flood stories from Genesis and the *Epic of Gilgamesh* using the excerpts in the chapter. Have them draw conclusions about why there are similarities and differences in these stories from people who lived so close to each other.

GEOGRAPHY CONNECTION

Interaction The Garden of Eden can be seen as reflecting the Israelites' belief in an ideal life at the beginning of time when humans did not have to work for a living. But humans disobeyed God and were punished by having to work to make or gather food. Ask students to describe the work that Adam and Eve would have had to do to survive, based on their knowledge of how early Near Eastern peoples adapted to the Near Eastern environment and subsequently adapted the environment to their own use.

READING COMPREHENSION QUESTIONS

1. What did the Israelites believe that Yahweh did for Adam and Eve? What was Yahweh's only requirement? How did that story end? (*Yahweh gave Adam and Eve everything in the world for their use, and all they had to do was obey him. But Adam and Eve ate the forbidden fruit, disobeying Yahweh, and had to leave the Garden of Eden and work for a living.*)
2. Why did they believe that Yahweh sent a flood to destroy humans? (*Yahweh was angry with the violent nature of humans.*)
3. According to the Israelites, why do people from different lands speak different languages? (*After the flood receded, Noah's family began a new era on*

earth. At first, everyone spoke the same language. When they began to build a huge tower reaching toward the heavens, Yahweh worried that the people would become proud and rebellious. Yahweh caused the people to speak different languages. Since they could no longer understand each other, they left the tower and scattered to different lands.)

CRITICAL THINKING QUESTIONS

1. Read the Wrtng Gts Esr sidebar on page 122. Take a sentence from the book and copy it, leaving out all the vowels. How easy or hard is it to understand? Why might the Phoenician writing system still have been easier to learn than cuneiform? *(Students should recognize that it is difficult to read because we are used to reading words with vowels, but that the Phoenician writing system, with its relatively few symbols, would have been much easier to learn than cuneiform, with its hundreds of symbols.)*

2. In the story of Joseph and the coat of many colors, who do you think should have the most blame for Joseph being sold into slavery: Joseph's father or Joseph's brothers? Why? *(Answers will vary.)*

SOCIAL SCIENCES

Economics   Use the story of Joseph and his brothers in Egypt as a springboard to have students investigate the dislocation of farming societies during protracted droughts. Have partners find out about modern situations of famine for entire communities. Students can prepare oral reports including the details of the famine as well as relief measures.

READING AND LANGUAGE ARTS

Reading Nonfiction   Draw attention to the creation story from Genesis (page 120). Many peoples have their own versions of how the world began. Encourage students to research a creation story from another culture.

Using Language   Remind students that proper nouns such as names of people, countries, wars, battles, rivers, and places are capitalized. Have students list the proper nouns they find in part of the chapter and sort them into categories.

SUPPORTING LEARNING

English Language Learners   Have students read aloud with a partner one or more of the stories in the chapter. Have partners ask each other questions to review the material and then take turns retelling the story in their own words.

Struggling Readers   Have students complete a T-chart (at the back of this guide) for one or more of the stories in this chapter.

EXTENDING LEARNING

Enrichment   Have students use a Venn diagram (at the back of this guide) to compare the flood story in this chapter with the flood story in the Gilgamesh epic at *http://alexm.here.ru/mirrors/www.enteract.com/jwalz/Eliade/159.html*

Extension   Invite groups to create a storyboard for a story in this chapter: Adam and Eve, Noah and the flood, or the Tower of Babel.

VOCABULARY

genesis beginning or birth

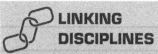

LINKING DISCIPLINES

Art Have students make three-dimensional representations of the Biblical stories mentioned in the chapter.

WRITING

Summary Have students summarize in their own words the sequence of stories from the creation of the earth until Joseph and his brothers lived in Egypt.

COMPARING RELIGIONS

Directions

Use the chart to compare and contrast the religion of the Israelites with the religion of Mesopotamians. Review Chapter 5 for information about Mesopotamian religion. For each characteristic, describe the beliefs of each religion.

Characteristic	Israelites	Mesopotamians
Number of gods		
What god (or gods) wants from humans		
Personality of god or gods		
Why humans were created		
What happened to humans if they angered god		

NAME _____ **DATE** _____

A. MULTIPLE CHOICE

Circle the letter of the best answer for each question.

1. Genesis, the first book of the Hebrew Bible, opens with a poem about
   a. a great flood.
   b. the creation of the world.
   c. the Tower of Babel.
   d. Abraham.

2. The Hebrew flood story involving Noah is similar to a Mesopotamian flood story involving
   a. Hammurabi.
   b. Sargon.
   c. Enkidu.
   d. Ut-napishtim.

3. The Israelites' god, Yahweh, combined the traits of the Mesopotamian gods
   a. Enlil and Shamash.
   b. Enlil and Ea.
   c. Ea and Adad.
   d. Ea and Ishtar.

4. The Israelites believed that Yahweh had made people speak different languages so that they would not
   a. become proud and rebellious.
   b. be too close to each other.
   c. build tall buildings.
   d. destroy the earth.

5. According to the story of Joseph, the Israelites were welcomed into Egypt because Joseph
   a. led them there.
   b. became a powerful man in Egypt.
   c. was hated by his brothers.
   d. asked them to come.

B. SHORT ANSWER

Write one or two sentences to answer each question.

6. What part did Noah play in the Israelite story of the great flood?

   _____

   _____

7. According to tradition, how are the Israelites and Arabs related to each other?

   _____

   _____

8. What does the story of Joseph teach about relationships between family members?

   _____

   _____

C. ESSAY

On a separate sheet of paper, write an essay summarizing the Israelites' stories about the creation of the world and of human beings.

CAST OF CHARACTERS

Josiah (jo-SIE-ya) king of Judah (639–609 BCE) who reformed Israelites' religious practices

Moses biblical personality who led Israelites out of slavery and received the Ten Commandments

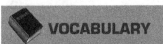

VOCABULARY

scroll rolled document

Exodus departure; refers to the Israelites departure from Egypt

absolute laws laws that never change, even if conditions change

CHAPTER SUMMARY

Israelites living in Judah long after Solomon's death rediscovered a book of ancient laws that included the Ten Commandments. These laws have been important to the Jews ever since. The book became part of the Hebrew Bible. The book said that Yahweh had given the laws to Moses during the Exodus (the Israelites' escape from Egypt). They included guidelines for how to worship Yahweh and how to live virtuously. Other laws gave rules for ceremonies and rituals, and some governed daily life. The main theme of the Hebrew Bible is that Yahweh rewarded those who followed his laws and punished those who disobeyed them.

PERFORMANCE OBJECTIVES

▶ To understand the Israelite laws
▶ To understand the connection between Yahweh and the laws

BUILDING BACKGROUND

Elicit from students their knowledge of the Ten Commandments, and ask how they know this. (*general knowledge, religious education*) Draw out that these are absolute laws—they don't change—not conditional laws that depend on circumstances. This was an important development in the history of law.

WORKING WITH PRIMARY SOURCES

The full text of Deuteronomy is available in many translations on the Internet and in print. One source is *www.ewtn.com/library/scriptur/deuteron.txt.* Chapter 5 of the book lists and expands on the Ten Commandments. Other chapters lay down the laws the Israelites were supposed to follow. The text of the book may be difficult for some students to understand. Read excerpts from the book as a class to learn more about the laws.

GEOGRAPHY CONNECTION

Location   The chapter does not identify the mountain on which Moses received the Ten Commandments from Yahweh, although it is commonly referred to as Mt. Sinai. In fact, the location of such a mountain is in dispute. For centuries, people believed that Mt. Sinai was in the Sinai Peninsula, midway between Egypt and the present-day Israel. However, there is no direct archaeological evidence for this. Interested students can investigate the controversy over this matter online or in other archaeological sources.

READING COMPREHENSION QUESTIONS

1. According to the Bible, who was Moses? What did he do for the Israelites?
   (*Moses was born to an Israelite woman in Egypt who hid him so he would not be killed, and then placed him in a basket in the Nile, where he was found and raised by the pharaoh's daughter. Moses pled with the pharaoh to free his people,*

and with divine intervention managed to lead the Israelites out of Egypt and to Canaan. On the way, Moses received the Ten Commandments from Yahweh.)

2. How did King Josiah's discovery of the Book of Deuteronomy affect the Israelites? *(It reminded them to worship one god; gave them laws to follow; and gave them an explanation—not following the laws—of why terrible things had happened to them.)*

3. What effect did the biblical laws have on later people? *(Other people read the laws and wrote commentaries on them, and these ideas were passed on to later generations. The importance of living under a set of laws is now a basic principle for most modern countries.)*

4. How do scholars know that more than one person wrote the books of the Bible? *(They used different styles of writing, and called God by different names.)*

CRITICAL THINKING QUESTIONS

1. What is the difference between absolute laws and conditional laws? *(Absolute laws do not change from situation to situation. For example, the sixth commandment says simply, "You shall not kill." A conditional law applies when certain conditions occur. For example, if one person has a dispute with another person, how shall the dispute be resolved.)*

2. Why does the chapter call monotheism "one of the Israelites' most important contributions to world history"? *(All modern Jews, Christians, and Muslims believe in a single god. So the beliefs of hundreds of millions of people sprang from the Israelites' belief.)*

SOCIAL SCIENCES

Civics   Distribute copies of the blackline master for Chapter 20 so students can learn more about the laws in the Book of Deuteronomy.

READING AND LANGUAGE ARTS

Reading Nonfiction   Point out the Historian at Work feature on page 130 and discuss the convention of using different type styles to indicate questions and answers. Have students read the interview aloud, taking turns reading a question and an answer. Discuss what the interview adds to the book.

Using Language   Write *monotheist* and *polytheist* on the board. Elicit the meanings of *mono-* ("one") and *poly-* ("many"). Have students name and define other words that begin with these prefixes.

SUPPORTING LEARNING

English Language Learners   In small groups, have students read sections of the text to each other and take notes.

Struggling Readers   Have students compare and contrast the laws in Deuteronomy and the Ten Commandments (pages 128, 131).

EXTENDING LEARNING

Enrichment   Have a group of students present to the class the words to the spiritual, "Go Down Moses," a religious song sung by slaves in the American South, online at *www.negrospirituals.com/ news-song/go_down_moses2.htm*. Discuss the song's ties to the Exodus story.

Extension   Students can prepare a choral reading of Exodus, Chapter 2, verses 1–10, in the Hebrew Bible (*www.mechon-mamre.org/e/et/et0202.htm*).

LINKING DISCIPLINES

Health Have students write and illustrate the Ten Commandments of Health, or absolute laws to follow to live a healthy life. Students can find helpful information about teen health issues online at *www.teenshealth. org/teen/*, a website created by the Nemours Foundation.

WRITING

In Their Own Words Have students rewrite the Ten Commandments in their own words and give examples that explain the meanings of the commandments.

NAME   DATE

THE LAWS OF DEUTERONOMY

Directions

Read these excerpts from the Book of Deuteronomy. Then answer the questions about the laws.

> ▶ If there be a controversy between men, and they call upon the judges: they shall give the prize of justice to him whom they perceive to be just: and him whom they find to be wicked, they shall condemn of wickedness.
> ▶ And if they see that the offender be worthy of whipping: they shall lay him down, and shall cause him to be beaten before them. According to the measure of the sin shall the measure also of the whipping be.
> ▶ When brothers dwell together, and one of them dies without children, the wife of the deceased shall not marry to another: but his brother shall take her, and raise up children for his brother.
> ▶ And the first son he shall have of her he shall call by his name, that his name be not abolished out of Israel.
> ▶ Thou shalt not have different weights in thy bag, a greater and a less.
> ▶ Neither shall there be in thy house a greater bushel and a less.
> ▶ Thou shalt have a just and a true weight, and thy bushel shall be equal and true: that thou mayest live a long time upon the land which the Lord thy God shall give thee.
> ▶ For the Lord thy God abhors him that does these things, and he hates all injustice.

1. What do the first two laws say about resolving disagreements between people?

_____

_____

_____

2. What do the second two laws say about the importance of family?

_____

_____

_____

3. What do the third three laws say about honesty in business?

_____

_____

_____

NAME **DATE**

A. MULTIPLE CHOICE

Circle the letter of the best answer for each question.

1. King Josiah was so upset when his secretary read the scroll because he knew that the Israelites
   a. were about to be invaded. **c.** had not paid their taxes.
   b. had forgotten Yahweh's laws. **d.** could not read.

2. According to the Hebrew Bible, Moses did all of the following **except**
   a. lead the Israelites out of slavery. **c.** become the first king of Israel.
   b. lead the Israelites to Canaan. **d.** give the Israelites the Ten Commandments.

3. King Josiah was most concerned with following the first of the Ten Commandments, which is about
   a. worshiping Yahweh. **c.** stealing.
   b. observing the Sabbath. **d.** telling lies.

4. The laws of the Ten Commandments are
   a. conditional laws. **c.** absolute laws.
   b. changeable laws. **d.** scientific laws.

B. SHORT ANSWER

Write one or two sentences to answer each question.

6. Why was belief in the Exodus from Egypt important to Israelites?

_____

_____

7. How can we tell that the Bible stories were written down in different times?

_____

_____

8. How did Josiah's reforms eventually change the Israelites' beliefs about Yahweh?

_____

_____

C. ESSAY

Write an essay on a separate sheet of paper describing how scholars study a biblical text.

UNIT OBJECTIVES

Unit 7 discusses the great empires that arose to unify the Near East from the 10th century BCE until the arrival of Alexander in the 4th century BCE. In this unit, your students will learn

► how the Assyrians conquered and ruled the region.
► how the Babylonians reasserted their power in a short-lived but strong empire.
► how the Israelite religion managed to survive Judah's conquest by the Babylonians.
► how the Persians created the largest empire known to that time.
► why the Near Eastern cultures were mostly forgotten after Alexander's conquest.

PRIMARY SOURCES

Unit 7 includes excerpts from the following primary sources:

► Ashurnasirpal II, Royal inscription
► Assyrian inscription on obelisk
► II Kings, Hebrew Bible
► Sennacherib, royal inscription
► Cuneiform document, 7th century BCE
► Babylonian Chronicle
► Ration list, 6th century BCE
► Psalms, Hebrew Bible
► Adad-Guppi, Autobiography
► Nabonidus, Royal inscription
► Temple program for the New Year's Festival, Babylon
► "Cyrus Cylinder" inscription
► Herodotus, *Histories*
► Isaiah, Hebrew Bible

Pictures of Near Eastern artifacts about the great empires studied in this unit can also be analyzed as primary sources.

► Relief from Ashurnasirpal II's palace at Calhu
► Relief of chefs and priests in an army camp
► Relief of King Jehu of Israel and Shalmaneser III of Assyria
► Wall painting of Assyrian officials
► Glazed brick lion from Babylon's Processional Way
► Ishtar Gate into Babylon, now in a museum in Germany
► Neo-Babylonian onyx sceptre

- ▶ Priest on clay seal
- ▶ Glazed brick dragon on Babylon's Ishtar Gate
- ▶ Painting of Croesus, Greek vase
- ▶ Darius's Inscription at Bisitun
- ▶ Remains of King Darius's palace at Persepolis
- ▶ Glazed brick images of archers, Darius's palace
- ▶ Pythagorean theorem on Mesopotamian tablet
- ▶ Phoenician coin

BIG IDEAS IN UNIT 7

Conflict, government, and **religion** are the big ideas presented in Unit 7. The unit begins with the rise of the Assyrian empire and the organization of its government, and then describes how Babylonia reasserted its power and the role of religion during its short revival. Finally, it describes the rise and fall of the Persian Empire and the legacy of the Mesopotamians.

One way to introduce these ideas is to reach back to the first Mesopotamian empire of Sargon, and to remind students of its size, its organization, and its religion. Have students use maps in the book to compare the size of these later empires with that of Sargon, and help them understand that, although the later empires were much larger than Sargon's, they had many similarities.

GEOGRAPHY CONNECTION

Elicit from students that although some earlier Near Eastern kingdoms were quite large, none of them extended beyond the region. Elicit a definition of *region* (an area that has a unifying characteristic, either natural or human). Display a map of the modern Middle East and show students that the empires they will now study encompassed peoples from several regions—from Greece and Egypt in the west to India in the east—and a multitude of cultures not experienced by the earlier kingdoms.

TIMELINE

10th century BCE	Assyria begins to expand
883–859 BCE	Ashurnasirpal II of Assyria reigns
842–815 BCE	King Jehu rules Israel
722 BCE	Assyrians crush rebellion of Israelites
704–681 BCE	Sennacherib of Assyria rules largest empire in world
649–547 BCE	Adad-Guppi, mother of Nabonidus, lives
612 BCE	Nineveh destroyed; Assyrian Empire ends; Neo-Babylonian Empire begins
605–562 BCE	Nebuchadnezzar II of Babylonia reigns
585 BCE	Babylonians destroy Jerusalem, send Jews into exile
555–539 BCE	Nabonidus of Babylonia reigns
550 BCE	Cyrus of Persia conquers Medes; Persian empire stretches from Anatolia to India
547 BCE	Cyrus conquers Lydia
539 BCE	Cyrus conquers Neo-Babylonian Empire
522–486 BCE	Darius I of Persia reigns
490 BCE	Darius attacks Greece and is defeated
486–465 BCE	Xerxes of Persia reigns
480 BCE	Xerxes attacks Greece and is defeated
330 BCE	Alexander the Great conquers Persia

UNIT PROJECTS

Historical Map

Have a group of students create a historical map to show the ebb and flow of the later Near Eastern empires. Students should obtain an outline map of the region from Egypt to India, decide on a key to represent each empire, and then complete the map, labeling each empire with its name and years of existence.

Great Emperors

Have small groups each research a ruler mentioned in the unit: Ashurnasirpal, Sennacherib, Nebuchadnezzar, Croesus, Cyrus, Darius, and Xerxes. Have them create displays and oral reports to inform the class of what they found out about each ruler.

Great Empires

Have groups research the governments of the Assyrian and Persian empires and report in greater detail how these huge empires were governed. Individuals might investigate transportation in the empire, defending the borders, governors or provinces, how taxes were paid, and the role of religion.

ADDITIONAL ASSESSMENT

For Unit 7, divide the class into groups and have them all undertake the Great Emperors and Great Empires projects so you can assess their understanding of the empires and their rulers. Use the scoring rubric at the back of this guide to assess students' work, and have students rate their own work with the self-assessment rubric.

UNIVERSAL ACCESS

The following strategies are designed to cover a range of learning styles and reading, language, and skill levels. You may find that any of your students will benefit from various strategies presented.

Reading Strategies

▶ Have the class read the chapters aloud. Stop the reading from time to time and lead students in taking notes about the text.
▶ Have small groups read each chapter together. When they are done, one group member should act as the Questioner and ask questions about the text. Other group members should answer with details from the chapter.

Writing Strategies

▶ Have students imagine themselves as young members of one of the royal courts discussed in the unit. Ask them to write their reactions to the ruler.
▶ Have students complete comparison-contrast charts for the rulers discussed in the unit.

Listening and Speaking Strategies

▶ Ask volunteers to role-play the different personalities discussed in the unit. Have each student prepare information about the person, and have them come before the class and tell about themselves.

▶ Have partners write serial questions for each other to answer about the empires. One partner writes a question and passes it to the other. The second partner answers the question, and then writes back a different question on the same sheet.

UNIT VOCABULARY LIST

The following words that appear in Unit 7 are important for your students' understanding of the social studies content as well as for development of literacy. Use these words for vocabulary study or to reinforce language arts skills (e.g., synonyms, compound words, prefixes and suffixes, and related words). The words are listed below in the order in which they appear in the chapters.

Chapter 21	Chapter 22	Chapter 23	Chapter 24	Epilogue
warrior	dominate	scepter	windless	contrast
battering ram	curse	fortune	polish	eclipse
tribute	helpless	kingship	decipher	rediscover
empire	artificial	autobiography	heaven	levee
besiege	terrace	chaos	burial mound	reservoir
cabinet	surpass	preserved	province	foster
adviser	historian	mummy	ambitious	
station	captivity	propaganda	gymnasium	
	interpret	obsess		
	prophet	prosperity		
	besiege			
	Zion			

ASSYRIA'S FIGHTER KINGS: WARRIORS BUILD AN EMPIRE

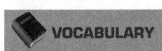

VOCABULARY

battering ram device used to smash through a city's defenses

Ashur Assyrian god who gave name to the people

CAST OF CHARACTERS

Ashurnasirpal II (ah-shur-NAH-zir-pahl) Assyrian king (883–859 BCE) who expanded his empire and build a great palace at Calhu

Sennacherib (sen-NAH-keh-rib) Assyrian king (704–681 BCE) who destroyed Babylon

CHAPTER SUMMARY

Neo-Assyrian kings, starting in the 10th century BCE, created a huge empire that incorporated much of the Near East. They adopted advanced military strategies and technologies that helped them prevail against many enemies. These are depicted in stone relief sculptures from the kings' palaces. The armies looted conquered cities, punished rebel leaders, and then imposed tribute on the cities: an annual payment that had to be made to the Assyrian king. Sometimes they deported whole populations, as they did in the case of the Israelites when Israel was conquered. The kings created an effective system of governing, using provincial governors and military outposts, and they kept in contact with all parts of their empire through letters carried by messengers.

PERFORMANCE OBJECTIVES

- ▶ To describe how the Assyrians built their empire
- ▶ To understand the extent of the Assyrian Empire
- ▶ To understand how the Assyrians administered their empire

BUILDING BACKGROUND

Read the chapter title and first paragraph of the chapter aloud, and have students match the narrative to the relief sculpture of Ashurnasirpal II attacking a city on the same page.

WORKING WITH PRIMARY SOURCES

Have students read Sennacherib's royal inscription about his destruction of Babylon in *The World in Ancient Times Primary Sources and Reference Volume* to learn how he dealt with rebellious cities, and the effect of his actions on people elsewhere.

GEOGRAPHY CONNECTION

Regions   Have students compare the map on page 135 to the maps on pages 111 and 115 to see which former kingdoms the Assyrians conquered.

READING COMPREHENSION QUESTIONS

1. Why was Ashurnasirpal attacking this city? (*The city had probably refused to pay the tribute money that Assyria demanded of its subjects. Ashurnasirpal was making an example of it for other cities.*)
2. What happened to Israel and Judah while under Assyrian rule? (*The two kingdoms paid tribute for many years, but then Israel rebelled. In 722 BCE, Assyria crushed the rebellion and sent many Israelites into exile. Judah continued to pay tribute.*)
3. How did Assyria control its huge territory? (*It had a well-organized government. The king took advice from experts. Governors ruled the major cities of the empire, sending reports and taxes to the king, drafting soldiers for the*

army, and keeping roads safe for travelers. Troops were stationed throughout the empire for quick military action.)

CRITICAL THINKING QUESTIONS

1. How would the Assyrians' belief that a man's duty was to be strong, brave, and warlike have helped them build a huge empire? *(Having that belief would make the Assyrian army very difficult to defeat in battle, and would probably influence the Assyrians to go to war more frequently. Knowing their reputation, other kingdoms would be less likely to oppose them.)*

2. Why do you think the people of Israel passed from history, while the people of Judah did not? *(Possible answer: The Israelites lost their king and probably gave up their belief in Yahweh, and so lost their identity. The people of Judah maintained their belief in Yahweh and continued to write down their history.)*

SOCIAL SCIENCES

Civics   Distribute copies of the blackline master for Chapter 21 and have students compare government in the Assyrian Empire to government in the United States.

READING AND LANGUAGE ARTS

Reading Nonfiction   Have students look at the map on page 135 and identify the kingdoms and cities the Assyrians conquered. Then explain that natural borders are boundaries that are based on natural features: rivers, oceans, mountain ranges, and so on. Have students identify the natural borders of the Assyrian empire.

Using Language   This chapter uses vivid adjectives and verbs on pages 133–134 to describe the Assyrian king and his warriors. Have students find examples of these adjectives and verbs and tell how these words affect their understanding.

SUPPORTING LEARNING

English Language Learners   Explain that the ending *-an*, as in the word *Assyrian*, shows that a person is "of a place." Ask students to name the people of Egypt, Babylonia, Mesopotamia, and America using this rule of thumb.

Struggling Readers   Have students create a main idea map graphic organizer (see reproducibles at the back of this guide) with *Assyrian Government* in the central circle. Have students use their completed charts to assess the statement on page 137 that "Assyria . . . had a well-organized system of government."

EXTENDING LEARNING

Enrichment   Have a group find out more about Ashurnasirpal's palace at Calhu and take a virtual tour of the throne room at *www.learningsites.com/NWPalace/NWPalhome.html*, a site recommended on the Websites page of the students' book. Students who visit the site can report their findings to the class.

Extension   Later civilizations copied the empire-ruling techniques of the Assyrians. Have a group of students create the Assyrian Empire Rules, a brochure, video, or oral presentation promoting the Assyrians' tried-and-true methods of controlling a far-flung empire.

WRITING

○ **Description** Have students write a short description of the city in the beginning of the chapter after it was destroyed by Ashurnasirpal. They should include sights, sounds, and smells.

LINKING DISCIPLINES

Art Have students illustrate scenes from the chapter, such as Ashurnasirpal's feast after his palace was finished or King Jehu bringing Israel's tribute to Shalmaneser III.

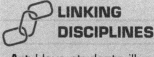

THEN and NOW

The last great Assyrian king, Ashurbanipal, assembled a library that held more than 20,000 tablets. Many of the tablets can now be found in the British Museum. Students can find more information about the library online at *http://en.wikipedia.org/wiki/Ashurbanipal*

ASSYRIAN GOVERNMENT VERSUS
UNITED STATES GOVERNMENT

Directions

Use the chart to compare and contrast features of the government of the Assyrian Empire with features of government in the United States.

Feature	Assyrian Empire	United States
Who leads the country		
Who advises the leader		
Who makes laws		
Who governs local regions		
How laws are enforced throughout country		
How government operations are paid for		
How country deals with foreign countries		

A. MULTIPLE CHOICE

Circle the letter of the best answer for each question.

1. After a rebellious city was defeated and its walls broken, Assyrian soldiers could
   a. go back to their homes.
   b. take some of the wealth of the city.
   c. marry the women of the city.
   d. stay and live in the city.

2. The tribute paid to the Assyrian king by conquered cities guaranteed protection from
   a. enemies as well as the Assyrians.
   b. extra taxes.
   c. earthquakes.
   d. angry gods.

3. The Assyrians' reputation for brutality in war made some cities
   a. harder to defeat.
   b. less of a prize.
   c. give up without a fight.
   d. stop building walls.

4. If a city peacefully submitted to Assyrian rule, the Assyrians might have
   a. destroyed the city anyway.
   b. not demanded any tribute.
   c. left its gods alone.
   d. allowed the king to keep his throne.

5. At its peak, the Assyrian Empire was
   a. almost as large as Sargon's empire.
   b. the largest empire the world had seen.
   c. about the size of Africa.
   d. as large as Egypt.

B. SHORT ANSWER

Write one or two sentences to answer each question.

6. What was the source of Assyrian wealth?

_____

_____

7. What happened to Israel after it rebelled against Assyrian rule in 722 BCE?

_____

_____

8. How did Assyria influence rulers of later empires?

_____

_____

C. ESSAY

On a separate sheet of paper, write an essay explaining how the Assyrians were able to control their huge empire.

A BRIGHT STAR SHINES— BRIEFLY: BABYLON RISES, JUDAH FALLS

CAST OF CHARACTERS

Nebuchadnezzar II (NEB-yoo-kad-NEZ-er) Neo-Babylonian king (605–562 BCE) who expanded empire, conquered Judah

Jehoiachin (je-HOY-ah-keen) last king of Judah (598–597 BCE)

Herodotus (huh-RAH-duh-tus) 5th-century BCE Greek historian

Daniel described in Hebrew Bible as 6th-century BCE Jewish holy man who survived in a den of lions

CHAPTER SUMMARY

The Neo-Assyrian empire came to an end in 612 BCE when it was conquered by its enemies, including Babylon. The Neo-Babylonian rulers included Nebuchadnezzar, who took over most of the Neo-Assyrian empire and conquered Judah, the last remaining home to the Israelites. The Judeans were exiled to Babylon, where they began putting together the books of the Bible, and where many of the Psalms were written. Babylon was built up and beautified during Nebuchadnezzar's reign, with huge city walls and a grand ziggurat dedicated to the god Marduk.

PERFORMANCE OBJECTIVES

▶ To understand how power changed in the Near East in the 7th century BCE
▶ To understand that subject kingdoms still strove for independence
▶ To visualize the wonders of the city of Babylon

BUILDING BACKGROUND

Elicit students' knowledge of cities that are revitalizing themselves by planning and building new downtown areas, fixing up public buildings, and creating visionary parkland. Explain that such renovation, whether paid for by public or private sources, costs hundreds of millions of dollars. What is the effect of such developments on visitors to those cities? What benefits do the workers and residents of those cities realize?

WORKING WITH PRIMARY SOURCES

There are numerous translations of the Psalms available, in print and online. Have students read a variety of Psalms to draw conclusions about the beliefs of the people who wrote them. One source of Psalms, in Hebrew and English, is *www.mechon-mamre.org/p/pt/pt0.htm.*

GEOGRAPHY CONNECTION

Location Refer students to the map on page 148, and have them estimate the distance from Jerusalem to Babylon. (Remind them not to measure in a straight line across the desert, but to follow the arc of Babylonian territory.) Elicit from students the limited world view of the Near Eastern inhabitants of the time to help them understand why the Jews thought they would never return to Jerusalem.

READING COMPREHENSION QUESTIONS

1. Why did the Assyrians handle Babylon carefully, even at the height of their power? (*Marduk, the most power of the Mesopotamian gods, was the god of Babylon, and the Assyrians did not want to risk being cursed by Marduk.*)
2. What happened to the kingdom of Judah when it rebelled against Nebuchadnezzar in 587 BCE? (*Nebuchadnezzar marched against Judah with his*

entire army and besieged Jerusalem for two years. The Babylonians finally broke through the walls and destroyed the city and its temple. They deported thousands of people from Judah to Babylon.)

3. Describe the city of Babylon during the reign of Nebuchadnezzar. *(Babylon was huge and elaborate. The Euphrates flowed through it. It was three miles square. The Processional Way crossed the city from Marduk's temple to the Gate of Ishtar. The seven story ziggurat dominated the skyline. It was a cosmopolitan city, with inhabitants from all over the empire.)*

4. Distribute copies of the blackline master for Chapter 22 and have students complete the activity.

CRITICAL THINKING QUESTIONS

1. Why do you suppose the people of Judah rebelled against the Babylonians in 597 and 587 BCE? *(They wanted their independence, as shown by the earlier rebellion against Assyria. They may have felt that the time was right, as Babylon had recently taken over a much weakened Assyria, and they may have thought they could defend themselves against Babylon.)*

2. Why was it important for the Jews that they maintained their belief in Yahweh while in exile in Babylon? *(Keeping their belief in their god meant that they kept their identity as a people.)*

SOCIAL SCIENCES

Economics   Page 143 states "The king spent a lot of the empire's wealth building up the cities of Babylonia. . . ." As students read the chapter, have them note what was built and figure out the kinds of workers that needed to be paid to build up the cities.

READING AND LANGUAGE ARTS

Reading Nonfiction   Explain that the chapter is organized into two sections—the rise of Babylon and the fall of Judah. Have students compare and contrast the fortunes of the two kingdoms by creating a two-column chart with the headings *Babylon* and *Judah* and listing information about their respective rise and fall.

Using Language   Write *exile, tribe, demolish,* and *rebellion* on the board. Have students define the words and then use them in original sentences.

SUPPORTING LEARNING

Struggling Readers   Have students use the outline graphic organizer (see reproducibles at the back of this guide) to track the rise of Babylon and fall of Judah.

EXTENDING LEARNING

Enrichment   Students can learn more about the Neo-Babylonian Empire and Nebuchadnezzar and see artifacts from Babylon at the British Museum's website. They can use the museum's search engine at *www.thebritishmuseum.ac. uk/compass/ixbin/hixclient.exe?_IXDB_=compass&search-form=graphical/main. html&submit-button=search* to find articles and pictures related to Nebuchadnezzar.

Extension   Have students design the front of a postcard showing a Babylonian site described in the chapter. Then ask students to write a postcard message about the site from a traveler in Nebuchadnezzar's time.

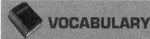

VOCABULARY

kid gloves soft gloves made from a young lamb or goat (kid); to "treat with kid gloves" means to be gentle with

Neo-Babylonian New Babylonian Empire; distinguished from Old Babylonian Empire in the 1700s BCE

Nebuchadnezzar's palace built higher than Hammurabi's palace, the later palace survived to be excavated by archaeologists

ziggurat terraced temple tower built in Mesopotamia and other ancient civilizations

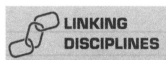

LINKING DISCIPLINES

Science Have a group of students investigate the city plan of Babylon, including the grid of streets, the defensive walls, the Processional Way and the major gates. Students can create their own maps of the city.

NAME

DATE

THE IDEA OF ANCIENT BABYLON

Directions
Read the excerpted text and answer the following questions. The complete text of Reverend King's sermon "I Am a Drum Major for Peace" can be found at *www.africanamericans.com/ MLKTheDrumMajorInstinct.htm*

Martin Luther King, Jr., was a clergyman and a civil rights leader who gained national prominence by supporting a policy of non-violent resistance to segregation. We celebrate Martin Luther King, Jr., Day as a national holiday on the third Monday in January every year.

> But God has a way of even putting nations in their place. The God that I worship has a way of saying, "Don't play with me." He has a way of saying, as the God of the Old Testament used to say to the Hebrews, "Don't play with me, Israel. Don't play with me, Babylon. Be still and know that I'm God. And if you don't stop your reckless course, I'll rise up and break the backbone of your power." And that can happen to America.

1. Martin Luther King's words are not those of everyday speech. How are they special or different? What words are unusual?

   _____

   _____

   _____

2. Martin Luther King seems to think Babylon is a bad place. Does anything in the chapter support his view of the city?

   _____

   _____

   _____

3. What connection does Martin Luther King make between Babylon and 20th-century America?

   _____

   _____

   _____

NAME   **DATE**

A. MULTIPLE CHOICE

Circle the letter of the best answer for each question.

1. Sennacherib's son rebuilt Babylon so that
   a. he would have a capital city.
   b. he could prove his father was wrong.
   c. Assyrian stonemasons would have work.
   d. the Assyrians wouldn't be cursed by Marduk.

2. Although the Assyrian and Babylonians were related to one another in many ways, they
   a. spoke different languages.
   b. had a different history
   c. worshiped different gods.
   d. fought to control the Near East.

3. After Nebuchadnezzar put down rebellions in Judah, he
   a. rebuilt Jerusalem.
   b. let the Jews worship at their temple.
   c. deported most of the Jews to Babylon.
   d. left the Jews alone.

4. The tallest structure in Babylon was
   a. Nebuchadnezzar's palace.
   b. the ziggurat of Marduk.
   c. the Ishtar Gate
   d. the Processional Way.

5. The Jews who were deported to Babylon wrote songs about
   a. war.
   b. accepting Babylonian gods.
   c. returning to Jerusalem.
   d. remaining in Babylon.

B. SHORT ANSWER

Write one or two sentences to answer each question.

6. How did Nebuchadnezzar spend most of his reign?

_____

_____

7. What did Nebuchadnezzar use much of the wealth of the empire to do?

_____

_____

8. Why would Babylon be an overwhelming city to someone who came from a small village in the Neo-Babylonian Empire?

_____

_____

C. ESSAY

Write an essay on a separate sheet of paper describing the fate of the Jewish people in the Neo-Babylonian Empire.

FOR HOMEWORK

STUDENT STUDY GUIDE

pages 55–56

CAST OF CHARACTERS

Adad-Guppi (ah-dahd-GOO-pee) 649–547 BCE; priestess of the moon good Sin and mother of King Nabonidus

Nabonidus (nah-boh-NIE-dus) last king (555–539 BCE) of Neo-Babylonian Empire

Cyrus (SIE-rus) king (559–530 BCE) of the Persian Empire who conquered Babylonia in 539 BCE

 VOCABULARY

desolate sad and disheartened

impurities objects or beliefs that make a religious setting unfit for ritual

humility being humble; accepting a lower rank

CHAPTER SUMMARY

The last king of Babylon was Nabonidus, a man who was not a member of the previous royal family. He and his mother, a priestess, were devoted to the god Sin (the moon god), rather than Marduk, the god of Babylon. This made him unpopular with the Babylonians. In 539 BCE Cyrus the Great of Persia used propaganda against Nabonidus to convince the Babylonians that they would be better off under Persian rule.

PERFORMANCE OBJECTIVES

▶ To explain the rise to power of Nabonidus, son of Adad-Guppi
▶ To analyze how Nabonidus lost favor amongst the Babylonians
▶ To understand the relationship between religion and kingship in Mesopotamia
▶ To understand the downfall of the Neo-Babylonian Empire at the hands of the Persians

BUILDING BACKGROUND

Remind students of the importance of a Mesopotamian city's god to its inhabitants, and what it meant to the city if the god was taken from the city or removed its favor from the city.

WORKING WITH PRIMARY SOURCES

Have a student read aloud the quotation from Cyrus on page 149, including the comments about the battle that Cyrus had to wage to conquer Babylon. Have students tell why a conqueror would issue a statement like this.

GEOGRAPHY CONNECTION

Movement   Refer students to the maps on pages 148 and 151. Explain that when Cyrus turned his attention to Babylonia, he had already conquered the Medes, whose empire had stretched from the Oxus River to Anatolia. Thus, the territory Cyrus commanded was already larger than Babylonia. Have students analyze what effect this would have on how Cyrus could have placed his armies to attack Babylonia.

READING COMPREHENSION QUESTIONS

1. How was Adad-Guppi able to rebuild her temple for Sin, the moon god? (*After many years, her son, Nabonidus, became king of Babylon. Whereas Nebuchadnezzar had ignored Harran, Nabonidus honored the moon god and rebuilt its temple.*)
2. Why might the people of Babylon have disliked Nabonidus? (*Since he honored the moon god, he didn't attend the New Year's festival for Marduk in Babylon for 10 years. The king's participation was essential for the festival, and for the people to feel they would prosper. The Babylonians would have resented Nabonidus for this.*)

3. How did Cyrus of Persia conquer the Neo-Babylonian Empire? (*He started a propaganda campaign against Nabonidus, saying that Marduk wanted him to rule over Babylonia. He promised to return Marduk to his rightful place. He fought a battle to overcome the forces of Nabonidus.*)
4. Distribute copies of the blackline master for Chapter 23 so students can compare and contrast the reigns of Nebuchadnezzar and Nabonidus.

CRITICAL THINKING QUESTIONS

1. Why do you think it was necessary for the king to submit to being slapped by the priest of Marduk? (*The Babylonians had to show respect for their god. The king, as leader of the people, had to symbolically show that the god was more powerful than he was.*)
2. The chapter says that "It's likely that most kings had the good sense to cry" after being slapped by Marduk's priest. Do you think the kings believed in the ritual, or did they cry just for show? (*Answers will vary.*)
3. In what ways were the religion and kingship closely connected in Babylon? (*The king thought he was chosen to rule by a god. The king was required to go through the New Year's ritual in order to assure the continued order of the universe, in their thinking. Kings felt that gods needed them to maintain and rebuild their temples.*)

SOCIAL SCIENCES

Civics   Have small groups brainstorm ideas for a perfect Babylonian city. Remind them of the important considerations of the time: defense against invaders, source of water, place to carry on trade, religion, government center, areas for tradespeople, organized street system, and so on.

READING AND LANGUAGE ARTS

Reading Nonfiction   Have students look at the map on page 151 and identify the natural borders of the Persian Empire, as well as the places mentioned in the chapter.

Using Language   Point out to students that this chapter is written in time order. Have students summarize the events in the chapter, using time-order words such as *first, next, then, later,* and so on.

SUPPORTING LEARNING

English Language Learners   Point out an example of a word with two meanings: *fortune* on page 146. Discuss what the word means in the phrases *cost a fortune* and *twist of fortune*. Have students use the word in original sentences.

Struggling Readers   Have students complete a T-chart graphic organizer (at the back of this guide) to better understand the connections between events in the chapter.

EXTENDING LEARNING

Enrichment   Students can view images of the Ishtar Gate at the Museum of the Ancient Near East website at *www.smb.spk-berlin.de/vam/e/s.html*.

Extension   Have students create a birthday poem or a speech to be recited at the 104th birthday celebration of Adad-Guppi. The work can touch on some of the things that were important to Adad-Guppi during her life.

WRITING

Dialogue Have partners write a dialogue between two announcers present at the king's ritual before Marduk at the New Year. The announcers should set the scene, tell who is there, and describe the action, including whether or not the king cries after being slapped. Have volunteers read their work aloud.

LINKING DISCIPLINES

Art Have students look at the mosaic-style brickwork in the pictures of the Processional Way and Ishtar Gate on pages 139, 144, and 149. Have students make paper mosaic copies of these works for display in class.

COMPARING NEO-BABYLONIAN RULERS

Directions

Complete the chart with details from Chapters 22 and 23 to compare and contrast two rulers of the Neo-Babylonian Empire: Nebuchadnezzar II and Nabonidus.

Point of Comparison	Nebuchadnezzar II	Nabonidus
Years of reign		
How became king		
Best known for		
Building projects undertaken		
Babylonians' opinion of his rule		
How rule ended		

NAME _____   DATE _____

A. MULTIPLE CHOICE

Circle the letter of the best answer for each question.

1. Adad-Guppi thought Nabonidus should rebuild the temple to the moon god because she
   believed that
   a. Sin spoke to her in a dream.
   b. a son must follow a mother's wishes.
   c. Sin was the king of all the gods.
   d. kingship was a gift of the god Sin.

2. Adad-Guppi's fortunes changed for the better when
   a. Nebuchadnezzar died.
   b. her son Nabonidus became king.
   c. she became priestess to Marduk.
   d. the New Year festival came to Harran.

3. Nabonidus was not typical of Babylonian kings because he
   a. believed in only one god.
   b. spoke Akkadian.
   c. only rarely lived in Babylonia.
   d. did not conquer any cities.

4. Babylonian opinion may have turned against Nabonidus because he did not
   a. attend the New Year festival for 10 years.
   b. keep the people well fed.
   c. worship Sin, the moon god.
   d. go to Babylonian schools.

5. The reign of Nabonidus ended when
   a. he was killed by his guards.
   b. he finally moved back to Babylonia.
   c. his mother died.
   d. Cyrus of Persia invaded.

B. SHORT ANSWER

Write one or two sentences to answer each question.

6. What did Mesopotamians believe it meant when a god appeared in someone's dreams?

_____

_____

7. Why was the New Year festival at Babylon important to the people?

_____

_____

8. What kind of propaganda did King Cyrus of Persia use against Nabonidus?

_____

_____

C. ESSAY

**On a separate sheet of paper, write an essay explaining how Cyrus took advantage of the
situation in Babylonia to make his conquest easier.**

CAST OF CHARACTERS

Croesus (KREE-sus) king of Lydia (560–547 BCE) known for his legendary wealth

Darius I (duh-RYE-us) Persian emperor (522–486 BCE) who built Persepolis and introduced coins

Zoroaster (ZOR-oh-ASS-ter) Persian religious teacher who founded Zoroastrianism

Xerxes (ZURK-seez) Persian emperor (486–465 BCE) who tried, but failed, to conquer Greece

Alexander the Great Macedonian king of the Greeks (356–321 BCE) who conquered the Persian Empire

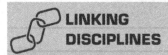

LINKING DISCIPLINES

Science/Math Have students do more research on Mesopotamian discoveries in astronomy, math, and boat building. They can display their findings on posters.

CHAPTER SUMMARY

The Persian Empire, founded by Cyrus the Great, became the biggest empire the world had ever seen. The Persian kings credited their successes to the god Ahura Mazda, the god of the Zoroastrian religion. The Persian kings built a grand capital city at Persepolis with the help of artists from across the empire. They tried to conquer the Greeks in the 5th century BCE but it was the Greeks, under Alexander the Great who, in 330 BCE, conquered the Persian Empire.

PERFORMANCE OBJECTIVES

▶ To understand life in the Persian Empire
▶ To analyze how the death of a language causes the loss of knowledge about a culture
▶ To recognize the technologies, ideas, and values that have come down to us from the Near Eastern people

BUILDING BACKGROUND

Have students think about the influences of the ancient Near Eastern civilization on our modern lives. From their studies, students should be able to list influences in farming, religion, writing, and government.

WORKING WITH PRIMARY SOURCES

As students read the quotations from Cyrus on page 152, have them analyze whether these were empty boasts or statements of fact.

GEOGRAPHY CONNECTION

Region   Have students look at the map on page 151 and estimate the dimensions of the Persian Empire. Elicit the physical features that would make travel across the region difficult. (*mountains, deserts*) Ask why such a huge and varied territory can be called a region. (*It is a cultural region: the people had similar languages, writing, religion, government, and economy.*)

READING COMPREHENSION QUESTIONS

1. What were the three greatest victories of the Persian king Cyrus? What lands did these victories give him? (*He conquered the Medes, and their huge empire that stretched from the Oxus River to Anatolia. He next conquered Lydia, one of the richest kingdoms in Anatolia. Finally, he conquered Babylonia and its wealthy center, Mesopotamia, which gave him control over the entire Near East.*)
2. What action of Darius allowed modern scholars to learn about the ancient Near Eastern civilizations? (*Darius had his accomplishments carved on a mountainside in three languages—Persian, Akkadian, and Elamite. This allowed scholars to decipher cuneiform, allowing them to read the tablets they found elsewhere in the Near East.*)
3. What ended the Persian Empire as well as the 1,200-year-old Mesopotamian civilization? (*The Greeks, under Alexander the Great, conquered the Persian empire in 330 BCE.*)

4. Distribute copies of the blackline master for Chapter 24/Epilogue and have students summarize the contributions that Mesopotamian civilization made to the human experience.

CRITICAL THINKING QUESTIONS

1. Summarize the teachings of the Persian teacher Zoroaster. (*Zoroaster taught that the god Ahura Mazda constantly fought against a demon called The Lie, that each person was responsible for choosing good over evil, and that all of history was the story of humans acting out the struggle of good and evil in their lives. Zoroastrians tried to live good lives to please Ahura Mazda.*)

2. Over the centuries, changes in rulers hadn't changed life much in the Near East. Why did the conquest by the Greeks cause radical changes? (*Alexander and the kings who followed him made Greek the official language, which caused the older languages to die off. The Greeks built new cities with temples to Zeus and Athena, which caused people to forget the old gods. Eventually, much of the ways of the older civilization were lost.*)

3. What do you think has been the most important concept we have inherited from the people of the ancient Near East? (*Answers will vary, but students should take into account the far-reaching effects of innovations such as use of the wheel, farming, law, writing, and monotheism.*)

SOCIAL SCIENCES

Civics Have students analyze how changing the language that a people speaks changes their culture. Students can list the changes in a chart.

READING AND LANGUAGE ARTS

Reading Nonfiction To keep track of the people mentioned in the chapter, have students create a character chart on which to record names and brief descriptions as they read.

Using Language There are many colloquialisms—expressions used in casual conversation—in the chapter: *dead wrong, tall tales, stinging defeat, cinch, earth-shaking,* and others. Have partners find these expressions and use context clues to explain their meaning to each other.

SUPPORTING LEARNING

English Language Learners Have students read and discuss the As Rich as Croesus sidebar on page 153. Have students use it in an original sentence and think of modern people whose names could be substituted for Croesus.

Struggling Readers Have students complete a sequence of events graphic organizer (at the back of this guide) using the timeline on page 155 as a guide.

EXTENDING LEARNING

Enrichment Invite a group of students to present the Pythagorean theorem, discovered by the Mesopotamians 1,000 years before the Greek mathematician, Pythagoras. They can find a demonstration of the theorem, at *www.geom.uiuc.edu/~demo5337/Group3/bball.html.*

Extension Invite students to create a skit in which Cyrus makes a speech based on quotations in the chapter, reeling off his titles and boasting about his generosity as a conqueror (page 152).

VOCABULARY

satrap governor of a province in Persian Empire

ambitious having a desire to achieve a large goal

Pythagorean Theorem formula used to calculate length of one side of a right triangle

WRITING

- **Fiction** Have students write a short fictional piece showing what it might be like to have new rulers change the language used for government, books, and the mass media.

THEN and NOW

In modern Iraq, which includes all of ancient Mesopotamia, 67 percent of the population lives in cities, and only 12 percent of the land can be farmed.

ANCIENT NEAR EASTERN CONTRIBUTIONS TO THE MODERN WORLD

Directions
Use this diagram to describe the elements of modern civilization that can be traced back to the people of the ancient Near East.

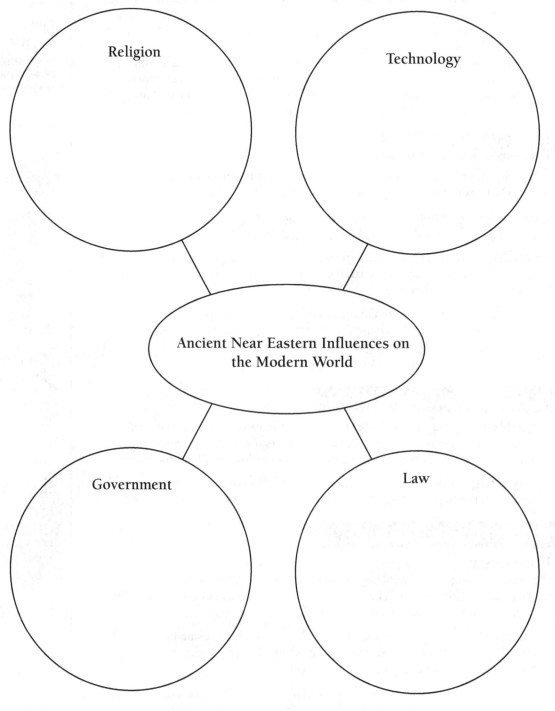

NAME _____ **DATE** _____

A. MULTIPLE CHOICE

Circle the letter of the best answer for each question.

1. After Cyrus established his empire, he says he tried to
   a. give his subjects a peaceful life.
   b. destroy the gods of his enemies.
   c. bring all his subjects to Babylon.
   d. make all his subjects worship Marduk.

2. Darius believed that the gods other people worshiped were
   a. false gods.
   b. gods that caused fear.
   c. just different names for Ahura Mazda.
   d. ineffective gods.

3. In order to govern effectively, Darius divided his empire into
   a. cities governed by kings.
   b. provinces governed by satraps.
   c. states governed by priests.
   d. territories governed by generals.

4. After Alexander the Great conquered the Persian Empire, life in the Near East changed because
   a. taxes increased.
   b. all of the cities were destroyed.
   c. Greek language and religion dominated.
   d. Mesopotamians were deported to Greece.

5. Elements of modern civilization that can be traced back to ancient Near Eastern cultures include all of the following **except**
   a. monotheism.
   b. democracy.
   c. laws that are fair for all people.
   d. coins.

B. SHORT ANSWER

Write one or two sentences to answer each question.

6. Where was Cyrus's original kingdom located?

_____

_____

7. What did Darius do so that people would remember him as one of the greatest kings of all time?

_____

_____

8. How could someone who cared for his family and obeyed the laws expect to be rewarded by

_____

_____

C. ESSAY

On a separate sheet of paper, write an essay describing a concept or innovation developed by ancient Near Eastern cultures and how it is reflected in modern society.

Directions

On a separate sheet of paper, answer each of the following questions.

1. Write an essay explaining how the Mesopotamians started farming and the innovations they used to grow more crops.

2. What are some important components of a civilization that developed in Mesopotamia during the Uruk period?

3. Draw and fill out a sequence chart like this one to show the steps in the development of writing.

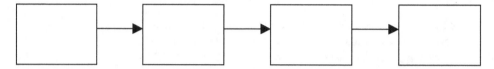

4. Write an essay describing the history and values that Mesopotamians were taught by *The Epic of Gilgamesh*.

5. Complete this chart with information about the law code of Hammurabi.

How it was made known to the Babylonians	
What kinds of cases it covered	
What kinds of punishments it handed out	
What it said about the court system	

6. Contracts were an important part of the Mesopotamian legal system. Write an essay discussing the kinds of agreements contracts were used for and the process by which contracts were finalized.

7. Use information from the book to complete a two-column chart about the advantages and disadvantages of royal marriages in the ancient Near East. Use sources from the palace at Mari as well as the letters of the five Great Kings.

8. Write an essay explaining how the Israelites differed from the other peoples of the Near East, and how these differences helped them throughout the centuries.

9. Use this Venn diagram to compare and contrast two great Near Eastern empires: the Assyrian Empire and the Persian Empire. Include information about the empires' origins, their religion, the lands they controlled, and how they were governed.

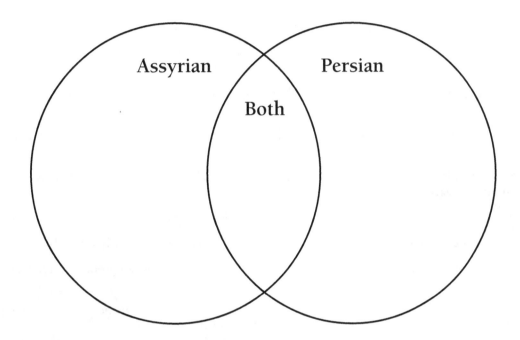

Assyrian   Persian

Both

10. The book says that, before Alexander the Great conquered Persia, life in Mesopotamia hadn't changed much for 1,200 years, but that Alexander's conquest changed things radically. Write an essay telling about those changes and explaining why the authors say that "the world of the ancient Mesopotamians had disappeared."

GRAPHIC ORGANIZERS

GUIDELINES

Reproducibles of seven different graphic organizers are provided on the following pages. These give your students a variety of ways to sort and order all the information they are receiving in this course. Use the organizers for homework assignments, classroom activities, tests, small group projects, and as ways to help the students take notes as they read.

1. Determine which graphic organizers work best for the content you are teaching. Some are useful for identifying main ideas and details; others work better for making comparisons, and so on.

2. Graphic organizers help students focus on the central points of the lesson while leaving out irrelevant details.

3. Use graphic organizers to give a visual picture of the key ideas you are teaching.

4. Graphic organizers can help students recall important information. Suggest students use them to study for tests.

5. Graphic organizers provide a visual way to show the connections between different content areas.

6. Graphic organizers can enliven traditional lesson plans and encourage greater interactivity within the classroom.

7. Apply graphic organizers to give students a concise, visual way to break down complex ideas.

8. Encourage students to use graphic organizers to identify patterns and clarify their ideas.

9. Graphic organizers stimulate creative thinking in the classroom, in small groups, and for the individual student.

10. Help students determine which graphic organizers work best for their purposes, and encourage them to use graphic organizers collaboratively whenever they can.

11. Help students customize graphic organizers when necessary; e.g., make more or fewer boxes, lines, or blanks, if dictated by the exercise..

OUTLINE

MAIN IDEA: _____

_____

_____

    DETAIL: _____

_____

    DETAIL: _____

_____

    DETAIL: _____

_____

MAIN IDEA: _____

_____

_____

    DETAIL: _____

_____

    DETAIL: _____

_____

    DETAIL: _____

_____

Name _____ Date _____

MAIN IDEA MAP

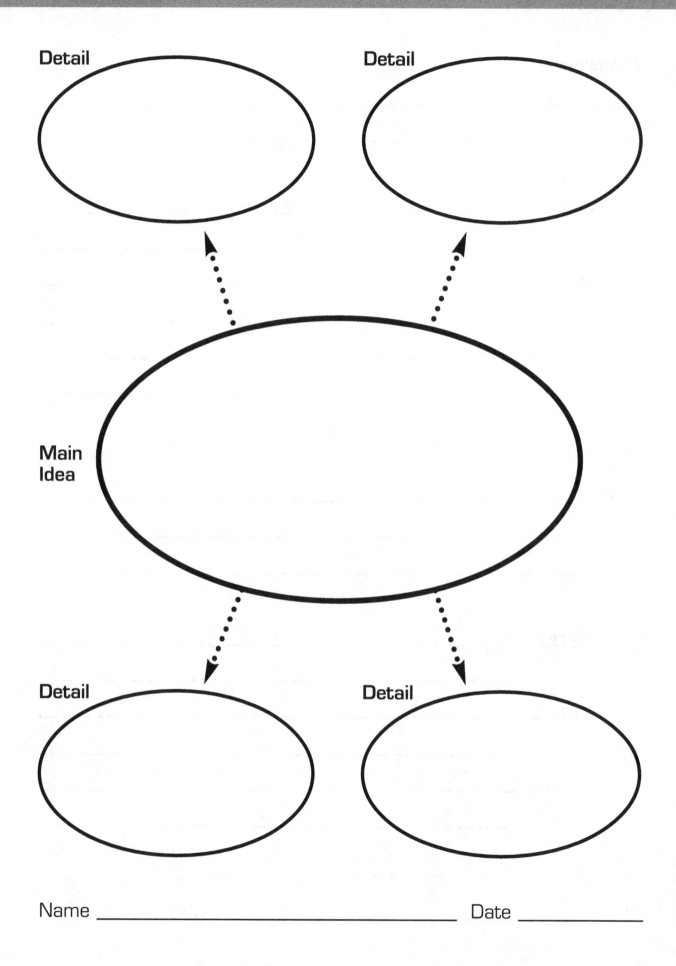

Detail

Detail

Main
Idea

Detail

Detail

Name _____ Date _____

K-W-L CHART

K	W	L
What I Know	What I Want to Know	What I Learned

Name _____

Date _____

VENN DIAGRAM

Write differences in the circles. Write similarities where the circles overlap.

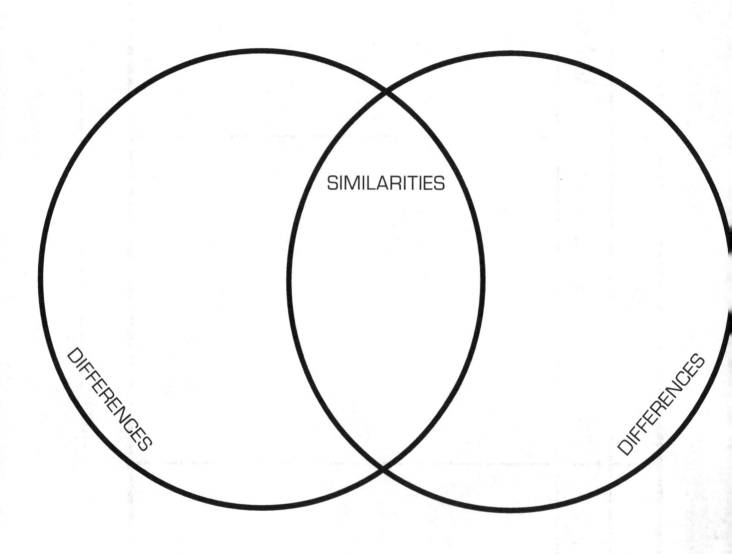

SIMILARITIES

DIFFERENCES

DIFFERENCES

Name _____ Date _____

TIMELINE

DATE

EVENT Draw lines to connect the event to the correct year on the timeline.

Name _____ Date _____

SEQUENCE OF EVENTS CHART

Event

Next Event

Next Event

Next Event

Next Event

Name _____ Date _____

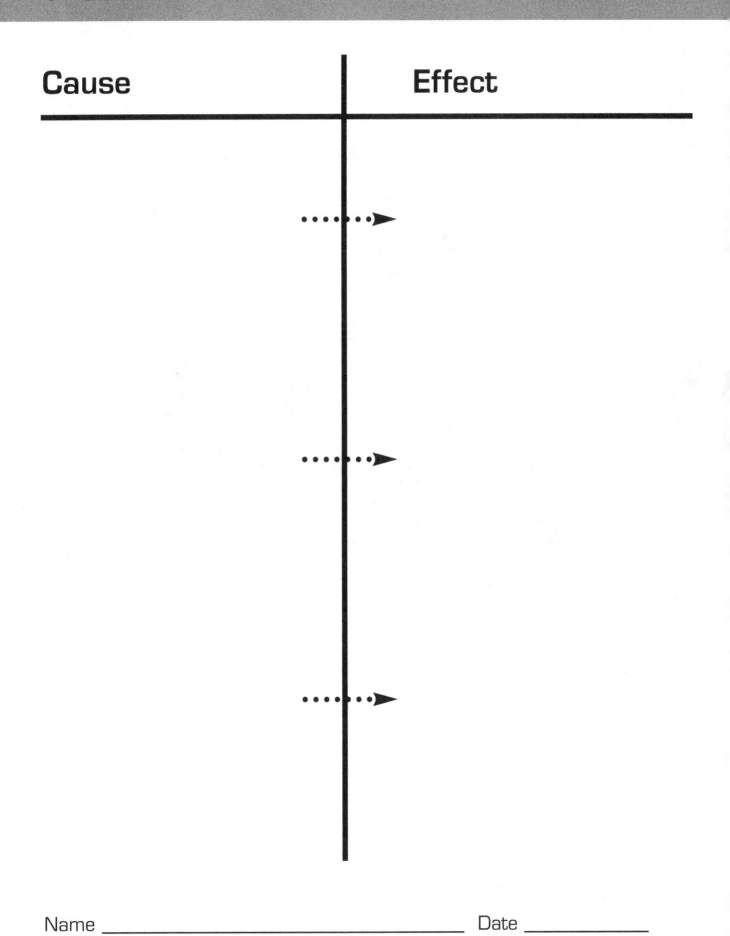

T–CHART

Cause	Effect

Name _____ Date _____

SCORING RUBRIC

The reproducibles on the following pages have been adapted from this rubric for use as handouts and a student self-scoring activity, with added focus on planning, cooperation, revision and presentation. You may wish to tailor the self-scoring activity—for example, asking students to comment on how low scores could be improved, or focusing only on specific rubric points. Use the Library/Media Center Research Log to help students focus and evaluate their research for projects and assignments.

As with any rubric, you should introduce and explain the rubric before students begin their assignments. The more thoroughly your students understand how they will be evaluated, the better prepared they will be to produce projects that fulfill your expectations.

	ORGANIZATION	CONTENT	ORAL/WRITTEN CONVENTIONS	GROUP PARTICIPATION
4	• Clearly addresses all parts of the writing task. • Demonstrates a clear understanding of purpose and audience. • Maintains a consistent point of view, focus, and organizational structure, including the effective use of transitions. • Includes a clearly presented central idea with relevant facts, details, and/or explanations.	• Demonstrates that the topic was well researched. • Uses only information that was essential and relevant to the topic. • Presents the topic thoroughly and accurately. • Reaches reasonable conclusions clearly based on evidence.	• Contains few, if any, errors in grammar, punctuation, capitalization, or spelling. • Uses a variety of sentence types. • Speaks clearly, using effective volume and intonation.	• Demonstrated high levels of participation and effective decision making. • Planned well and used time efficiently. • Demonstrated ability to negotiate opinions fairly and reach compromise when needed. • Utilized effective visual aids.
3	• Addresses all parts of the writing task. • Demonstrates a general understanding of purpose and audience. • Maintains a mostly consistent point of view, focus, and organizational structure, including the effective use of some transitions. • Presents a central idea with mostly relevant facts, details, and/or explanations.	• Demonstrates that the topic was sufficiently researched. • Uses mainly information that was essential and relevant to the topic. • Presents the topic accurately but leaves some aspects unexplored. • Reaches reasonable conclusions loosely related to evidence.	• Contains some errors in grammar, punctuation, capitalization, or spelling. • Uses a variety of sentence types. • Speaks somewhat clearly, using effective volume and intonation.	• Demonstrated good participation and decision making with few distractions. • Planning and used its time acceptably. • Demonstrated ability to negotiate opinions and compromise with little aggression or unfairness.
2	• Addresses only parts of the writing task. • Demonstrates little understanding of purpose and audience. • Maintains an inconsistent point of view, focus, and/or organizational structure, which may include ineffective or awkward transitions that do not unify important ideas. • Suggests a central idea with limited facts, details, and/or explanations.	• Demonstrates that the topic was minimally researched. • Uses a mix of relevant and irrelevant information. • Presents the topic with some factual errors and leaves some aspects unexplored. • Reaches conclusions that do not stem from evidence presented in the project.	• Contains several errors in grammar, punctuation, capitalization, or spelling. These errors may interfere with the reader's understanding of the writing. • Uses little variety in sentence types. • Speaks unclearly or too quickly. May interfere with the audience's understanding of the project.	• Demonstrated uneven participation or was often off-topic. Task distribution was lopsided. • Did not show a clear plan for the project, and did not use time well. • Allowed one or two opinions to dominate the activity, or had trouble reaching a fair consensus.
1	• Addresses only one part of the writing task. • Demonstrates no understanding of purpose and audience. • Lacks a point of view, focus, organizational structure, and transitions that unify important ideas. • Lacks a central idea but may contain marginally related facts, details, and/or explanations.	• Demonstrates that the topic was poorly researched. • Does not discriminate relevant from irrelevant information. • Presents the topic incompletely, with many factual errors. • Did not reach conclusions.	• Contains serious errors in grammar, punctuation, capitalization, or spelling. These errors interfere with the reader's understanding of the writing. • Uses no sentence variety. • Speaks unclearly. The audience must struggle to understand the project.	• Demonstrated poor participation by the majority of the group. Tasks were completed by a small minority. • Failed to show planning or effective use of time. • Was dominated by a single voice, or allowed hostility to derail the project.

NAME _____ **PROJECT** _____

DATE _____

ORGANIZATION & FOCUS	CONTENT	ORAL/WRITTEN CONVENTIONS	GROUP PARTICIPATION

COMMENTS AND SUGGESTIONS

UNDERSTANDING YOUR SCORE

Organization: Your project should be clear, focused on a main idea, and organized. You should use details and facts to support your main idea.

Content: You should use strong research skills. Your project should be thorough and accurate.

Oral/Written Conventions: For writing projects, you should use good composition, grammar, punctuation, and spelling, with a good variety of sentence types. For oral projects, you should engage the class using good public speaking skills.

Group Participation: Your group should cooperate fairly and use its time well to plan, assign and revise the tasks involved in the project.

NAME _____ **GROUP MEMBERS** _____

_____

_____

_____

Use this worksheet to describe your project by finishing the sentences below.
For individual projects and writing assignments, use the "How I did" section.
For group projects, use both "How I did" and "How we did" sections.

The purpose of this project is to :

Scoring Key =   **4** – extremely well
3 – well
2 – could have been better
1 – not well at all

HOW I DID

I understood the purpose and requirements for this project...

I planned and organized my time and work...

This project showed clear organization that emphasized the central idea...

I supported my point with details and description...

I polished and revised this project...

I utilized correct grammar and good writing/speaking style...

Overall, this project met its purpose...

HOW WE DID

We divided up tasks...

We cooperated and listened to each other...

We talked through what we didn't understand...

We used all our time to make this project the best it could be...

Overall, as a group we worked together...

I contributed and cooperated with the team...

NAME

LIBRARY/ MEDIA CENTER RESEARCH LOG

DUE DATE

What I Need to **Find**

I need to use:
☐ primary
☐ secondary
sources.

Places I **Know** to Look

Brainstorm: Other Sources and Places to Look

Rate each source from 1 (low) to 4 (high) in the categories below

helpful   relevant

WHAT I FOUND

Title/Author/Location (call # or URL)

How I Found it
Suggestion
Library Catalog
Browsing
Internet Search
Web link

Primary Source
Secondary Source

Book/Periodical
Website
Other

ANSWER KEY

CHAPTER 1

Blackline Master

Level 1 room of unbroken pottery; pieces of silver spearheads; four skeletons, two young women and two babies; gold, silver, lapis lazuli, bronze collar, iron necklace *Level 2* skeletons of two men; bronze dagger and spearhead; silver headband *Level 3* skeleton; silver cup; silver pins
1. They were buried with many valuable metal items made of gold, silver, bronze, iron, and lapis lazuli. 2. The women were royals, so lower-ranking men would be buried with them to serve them in the afterlife. 3. The Mesopotamians believed that you had to take gifts to the spirits who guarded the underworld.

Chapter Test

A. 1. c 2. a 3. b 4. a 5. b
B. 6. They analyze the style of the potsherds and the designs on them and match them with other remains that are of a known age to tell when a site was occupied. 7. Bone, stone, and clay are hard and do not disintegrate. Softer items, such as fabric fall apart. Objects made of valuable metal are reused and not discarded. 8. The farther down in the tell you excavate, the farther back in time you go.
C. Students' essays should indicate that there are many different jobs to do at an archaeological site, and many different types of knowledge needed.

CHAPTER 2

Blackline Master

The soil of southern Mesopotamia had no hard rocks to form river beds. After rivers flooded, they didn't always go back to the same path. *The people of southern Mesopotamia built levees.* They managed to keep the rivers flowing near their settlements for thousands of years. *Marshlands in southern Mesopotamia began to dry up.* The people of Eridu dug canals to bring water to their fields. *Families had more children and population grew.* Irrigation ditches were stretched farther to provide water for more land and more people. *The canal system expanded.* The fields became richer and the food supply grew. *Southern Mesopotamia developed good farming conditions.* More people were encouraged to settle near the southern towns. *Traders flocked to the growing villages in southern Mesopotamia to sell their wares.* This made the towns more interesting so more people would want to live near them. *Temples to the gods were built in the towns in southern Mesopotamia.* People wanted to live near their gods, increasing the population of the towns.

Chapter Test

A. 1. c 2. a 3. c 4. d 5. b
B. 6. Eridu is so far from water because the Euphrates River changed its course and the shore of the Persian Gulf has moved farther south. 7. Objects have been found in Eridu that could not have come from southern Mesopotamia. 8. Traders came to the towns of southern Mesopotamia because the towns had many people who were willing to trade.
C. Students' essays should include details about the development of irrigation and agriculture as well as the influence of traders and religion.

CHAPTER 3

Blackline Master

Potter's wheels helped Mesopotamians make more pots faster, giving them more things to trade. *Plows* allowed Mesopotamians to break up the hard, clay soil, helping to increase crops. *Bronze* allowed Mesopotamians to make strong plows, bowls, spearheads, other useful objects, and ornaments. *Spinning and weaving* allowed Mesopotamians to make trade goods with which they could get other items. *Wheeled carts* allowed Mesopotamians to carry greater amounts of goods farther in less time, promoting trade. *Cylinder seals* allowed Mesopotamian traders to label their goods and seal them against thieves

Chapter Test

A. 1. b 2. c 3. c 4. d 5. c
B. 6. The potters didn't have to spend much time farming because there were enough other people willing to trade food for pots. 7. The discovery of how to make bronze was important to Mesopotamian farmers because it allowed them to make plows that could break up the hard, clay soil. 8. By 3500 BCE, the Mesopotamians had cities, government, religious practices, specialized workers, long-distance trade, and social classes.
C. Students' essays should explain how innovations in pottery-making and farming led to increased trade, food production, population, and specialization.

CHAPTER 4

Blackline Master

Have students display their work, or trade it with other students.

Chapter Test

A. 1. d 2. c 3. a 4. b 5. c
B. 6. The first long-distance messages were clay tokens sealed in clay envelopes. 7. They let the use of the homonym determine its meaning. 8. Scribes used it to keep track of taxes and trade, contracts, lists of words, hymns, prayers, and royal inscriptions.
C. Students' essays should detail the steps in the evolution of Mesopotamian pictograms to simpler symbols and then to a syllabary.

CHAPTER 5

Blackline Master

1. Enheduanna seems to be describing a battle in heaven between the goddess Inanna and the other gods. 2. Inanna won the battle. 3. Enheduanna says Inanna is known by her size, her actions, her triumphs, and her countenance and flashing eyes. 4. Enheduanna will probably recite special prayers and make special sacrifices.

Chapter Test

A. 1. c 2. d 3. a 4. b 5. c
B. 6. The Mesopotamians thought that good things happened when the gods were happy with humans, and bad things happened when they were unhappy. 7. The gods became unhappy with Enlil because he didn't do any work and they had to do all the work to support him. 8. The Mesopotamians believed that if they served the goods well, good things would happen to them in this life.
C. Students' essays should indicate that the Mesopotamians' world view came from the area of the world that they could see around them or that they heard about from others who had traveled.

CHAPTER 6

Blackline Master

Gold and silver objects The society had wealthy people. It had people who could make beautiful objects out of gold and silver. *Cylinder seal with the words* Puabi, nin The society had royalty, since *nin* means "queen" in Sumerian. *Puabi's good teeth* The queen's diet didn't include too many sweets, and her bread did not have much rock dust in it. *Skeletons found in slumped positions* When royalty died, their attendants took poison and were buried with them.

Chapter Test

A. 1. c 2. a 3. b 4. a 5. b
B. 6. Puabi was probably the wife or mother of a king or a priestess with great power and wealth. 7. Archaeologists believe her attendants drank poison, and then were buried where they fell. 8. One possible way is that the *lugal* ("big man") served as ruler just during wartime, and then later began to rule full time.
C. Students' essays should indicate that kings could organize large building projects and defense of the city and lead troops against other cities.

CHAPTER 7

Blackline Master

Students' answers will vary but should be supported by details from *The Epic of Gilgamesh.*

Chapter Test

A. 1. d 2. a 3. b 4. c 5. a
B. 6. The Mesopotamians believe that the afterlife was a dark, grim place where people ate dirt. 7. The story of Gilgamesh was repeated orally over and over for 1,500 years, often sung at festivals and feasts. 8. Ut-napishtim saved himself, his family, and all the animals on earth from a flood sent by Enlil.
C. Students' essays should explain that Gilgamesh started out as a proud, self-centered young man, but his adventures turned him into a mature ruler of his people.

CHAPTER 8

Blackline Master

How Sargon created empire may have overthrown ruling king; set up new capital at Agade; conquered all the land from the Lower Sea to the Upper Sea. *Why Sargon created empire* perhaps to control the forest, mines, and other resources of the conquered lands. *Regions and cities conquered by Sargon* Sumer, Akkad, Upper Land; Ebla, Mari, Kish, Uruk, Lagash, Ur. *How Sargon ruled empire* Sargon probably sent his scribes as diplomats to foreign courts and the cities of his empire to bring messages and gifts and make Sargon's wishes known.

Chapter Test

A. 1. c 2. b 3. d 4. b 5. c
B. 6. Scholars can tell that Sargon probably was not from a royal family because Sargon would have named his father in his royal inscriptions if he had been a king. 7. Sargon prayed to foreign gods so that they would be on his side, too, in a battle. 8. They probably sent their scribes so the scribes could read messages and bring back replies.
C. Students should recognize that Ibubu was trying to express that he and the king of Hamazi, as well as Tira-il and the Hamazi scribe, were equal and friends.

CHAPTER 9

Blackline Master

Top officials of religions are appointed by religious groups. Top officials or religions were appointed by the king. *Religious organizations own land and buildings.* Religious organizations owned land and buildings. *Religious organizations hold festivals.* Religious organizations held festivals. *Religious organizations invite all people to prayer services.* Most worshippers were not even allowed inside the temples. *Religious organizations hire local workers to maintain their buildings, run their offices, and do other jobs not done by the leaders.* Religious organizations hired local workers to maintain their buildings and do other jobs not done by the leaders.

Chapter Test

A. 1. a 2. c 3. b 4. c 5. b
B. 6. To keep the gods happy, a priestess would sing hymns to its cult statue and place fine meals in front of it. 7. Nippur was the city of Enlil, who was ruler of the Mesopotamian gods. 8. A religious Mesopotamian would follow daily rituals, celebrate all public holy days, teach children and servants to honor the gods, and never swear to a false statement in front of a god.
C. Students' essays should mention that wealthy and poor Mesopotamians probably practiced religion in much the same way, except that the wealthy could afford to have small statues of themselves placed near the gods' statues in the temple.

CHAPTER 10

Blackline Master

1. These laws deal with false testimony, robbery, maintenance of public lands, and divorce. 2. The court wants to make sure that the person is telling the truth about what was stolen. 3. Law 138 tells what the husband has to do if he wants to divorce his wife. Law 148 says that a husband has to support a sick wife.

Chapter Test

A. 1. a 2. b 3. b 4. a 5. c
B. 6. People in Shulgi's time were not paid much money, and 15 shekels would represent more than a year's work for a laborer. 7. Hammurabi became an instant hero by canceling all debts and thus freeing all of those who had been sold into slavery. 8. Hammurabi's laws covered divorce, arguments over property, duties to the king, and criminal acts such as theft and assault.
C. Students' essays will vary, but their opinions should be supported with details from the chapter or reasoned arguments.

CHAPTER 11

Blackline Master

Students' contracts will vary. Have partners read their contracts to the class, and have the class discuss them.

Chapter Test

A. 1. b 2. c 3. c 4. c 5. b
B. 6. Hammurabi's laws cover specific situations, rather than telling people to "never" or "always" do something.
7. Mesopotamians used contracts for many situations, including adoptions, sales and rentals of houses and fields, marriages, purchases of slaves, and hiring workmen. 8. Judges used their judgement as well as guidance from the written laws.
C. Students' evaluations of the fairness of the contract will vary.

CHAPTER 12

Blackline Master

Students' answers will vary, but should be based on the information in the chapter.

Chapter Test

A. 1. c 2. c 3. c 4. d 5. a
B. 6. Their work was too noisy or smelly to be close to the palace.
7. The most important palace officials were paid for their work in

land, which they could then farm and make profits from the sale of the products. 8. Palace scribes kept records of all of the dealings of the palaces. The clay tablets that the records were written on have survived.

C. Students' essays should discuss the number of people who depended on the palace for their livelihoods, as well as the other trades and professions that brought wealth to many Mesopotamians.

CHAPTER 13

Blackline Master

The husband usually lived with his family and had to follow their traditions. The family helped him in his career; he generally followed his father's career. The wife lived with her husband's family, and helped care for the family's home. The wife still kept in touch with her family, and could get help from them or help them in times of distress. The husband and wife signed a marriage contract setting out the terms of the union as well as what would happen if they divorced. The husband provided income for the family, and the wife kept the household and tended to the children. The parents cared for the children, and were especially worried when they were sick.

Chapter Test

A. 1. a   2. a   3. d   4. c   5. a
B. 6. A woman controlled her dowry after she married because it was her inheritance from her parents and belonged to her. 7. A Mesopotamian woman was supposed to maintain contact with her family and help them out if they had trouble of some kind. 8. Mesopotamian boys generally chose the career that their fathers had.
C. Students' character sketches will vary.

CHAPTER 14

Blackline Master

1. a. 6 b. 15 c. 831 d. 109,395 2. Students should write the symbols for a. 5 tens and 4 ones b. 2 sixties, 2 tens, and 7 ones c. 37 sixties, 3 tens, and 1 one d. 15 thirty-six hundreds, 37 sixties, 3 tens, and 8 ones. 3. Answers will vary.

Chapter Test

A. 1. b   2. c   3. b   4. c   5. c
B. 6. An education allowed you to become a scribe, which meant you didn't have to do heavy labor and could be paid well for your services. 7. There were few female scribes. Those women who were scribes probably worked for priestesses. 8. The Mesopotamian number system is still seen in our seconds, minutes, and hours; in the 360-degree circle; and in using columns to indicate place value.
C. Students' essays should include the work the students did, the subjects they learned, and the punishments they received.

CHAPTER 15

Blackline Master

Health Shibtu wanted to keep her husband healthy. She had omens read about his health. *Royal household* Manged large staff, including weavers, leather workers, other laborers, and scribes. *Alliances* Zimri-Lim had to make alliances with neighboring kings. He might send his daughters to become wives of other kings to cement friendships. Sometimes these marriages didn't work out. *Family matters* Zimri-Lim had to advise his daughters who were living with other kings. Sometimes he told them to come home. *Official visits by ambassadors* Ambassadors had to be received, treated with respect, given a bath, listened to, and then honored at a feast. *Royal feasts* Feasts were huge affairs with special dishes and many servants.

Chapter Test

A. 1. a   2. c   3. b   4. d   5. a
B. 6. The king's daughter might have problems with other wives or might get treated poorly by her husband. 7. Zimri-Lim was kept informed by letters from his daughters, from his advisors and palace officials, from governors of cities within the kingdom, and from ambassadors to foreign courts. 8. The palace at Mari was probably two stories tall, with more than 300 rooms.
C. Students' essays should tell about alliances with some kingdoms, wars against others, and diplomacy.

CHAPTER 16

Blackline Master

Students' answers will vary. Have volunteers share their work with the class.

Chapter Test

A. 1. b   2. c   3. c   4. d   5. b
B. 6. The Hittites abandoned the city, taking its gods, its gold and silver, and many residents as slaves. 7. The Hittite state was weakened by palace plots and assassinations. 8. The fortunes of the Mesopotamians changed under the Kassites, who merged into the Mesopotamian society and strengthened the kingdom.
C. Students' essays will vary.

CHAPTER 17

Blackline Master

1. Mittani metals; Egypt gold; Hatti iron, timber; Babylon cloth; Alashiya copper 2. Have students show their work. 3. The "direct" route crosses the desert. It was much safer and easier to go up the coast of the Mediterranean and then down the Euphrates River.

Chapter Test

A. 1. b   2. d   3. c   4. a   5. d
B. 6. Egypt had different religious beliefs. They also had a different system of writing. 7. They were often at war because they were all trying to build empires on the same land. 8. By 1100 BCE, Mittani, Hatti, and Alashiya were gone, Egypt was struggling to survive, and trade had shriveled to nearly nothing.
C. Students' essays should include details about the diplomacy of the five Great Kings.

CHAPTER 18

Blackline Master

Various military rulers wars against neighboring peoples; were repeatedly defeated, would be better off with a king. *Saul* chosen by Israelites as first king, but defeated by Philistines; not a very effective king. *David* defeats the Philistine Goliath, unites the land under his control, rules over Canaanites, Hittites, Philistines, and Israelites, made Jerusalem the capital, builds palace; effective king and military leader. *Solomon* wise king, peaceful and profitable reign, traded with Phoenicians, built new palace and temple to Yahweh; effective king, kept the peace and enriched the country.

Chapter Test

A. 1. c   2. b   3. d   4. c   5. b
B. 6. Many Israelite authors wrote books about their people over hundreds of years. Eventually, editors put these texts into one book. 7. David became king of Israel after he was anointed by Samuel, defeated Goliath, and moved up in the ranks of the army. 8. Evidence for prosperity is Solomon building a new palace and a new temple, and trading with other countries.
C. Students' essays should include details about the history of Israel from the chapter.

CHAPTER 19

Blackline Master

Israelites: Number of gods 1; *What god (or gods) wants from humans* worship god by living good lives; *Personality of god or gods* Yahweh combined impatience with humans and protection of them; *Why humans were created* to live good lives; *What happened to humans if they angered god* bad things, like floods. *Mesopotamians: Number of gods* many; *What god (or gods) wants from humans* to serve and care for the gods; *Personality of god or gods* some gods could be impatient with humans, some were good to them; *Why humans were created* to care for the gods; *What happened to humans if they angered god* bad things, like floods.

Chapter Test

A. 1. b   2. d   3. b   4. a   5. b

B. 6. Noah built an ark and saved the animals and his family from destruction. 7. According to tradition, both peoples are descended from the sons of Abraham the Israelites from Isaace and the Arabs from Ishmael. 8. The story of Joseph teaches that people sometimes get along but sometimes fight, just as siblings in some families do.

C. Students' essays will vary but should include details from the chapter.

CHAPTER 20

Blackline Master

1. Judges should judge the two parties who are arguing according to which is just and which is wicked, and the wicked one should be whipped if he deserves it. 2. The family is very important; if one brother dies, the other should marry his wife and raise his children as his own. 3. Merchants should not use false weights and measures.

Chapter Test

A. 1. b   2. c   3. a   4. c   5. c

B. 6. Belief in the Exodus was important because it gave the Israelites a feeling of being a separate and united people. 7. We can tell the Bible stories were written in different times because of differences in style and because writers at different times mentioned people and events from their own times. 8. Josiah's reforms eventually got Israelites to believe that Yahweh as the only God and that he ruled over all peoples (monotheism).

C. Students' essays should give facts from the Historian at Work feature in the chapter.

CHAPTER 21

Blackline Master

Assyria: Who leads the country Emperor; *Who advises the leader* advisers and scribes; *Who makes laws* Emperor; *Who governs local regions* governors rule major cities; *How laws are enforced throughout country* Assyrian army; *How government operations are paid for* tribute money and gifts from other countries, money from military campaigns. taxes; *How country deals with foreign countries* goes to war against them.
United States: Who leads the country President; *Who advises the leader* Cabinet officers, other advisers; *Who makes laws* Congress (representatives of the people); *Who governs local regions* governors govern states; *How laws are enforced throughout country* laws are enforced by police and courts; *How government operations are paid for* people pay taxes; *How country deals with foreign countries* sends ambassadors, sometimes goes to war.

Chapter Test

A. 1. b   2. a   3. c   4. d   5. b

B. 6. Assyrians got wealth from tribute money paid by neighboring states and gold and silver taken from conquered states. 7. The Assyrians crushed the Israelite rebellion, imprisoned their king, and forced countless Israelites into exile. The kingdom of Israel ceased to exist. 8. Rulers of later empires copied Assyria's methods of controlling its empire provinces ruled by governors, troops stationed all over the empire, swift military action to put down rebellions.

C. Students' essays should include details about how the Assyrians controlled their empire, such as collecting tribute, crushing rebellions, and rewarding cooperative leaders by keeping them in power.

CHAPTER 22

Blackline Master

1. King's words are taken from a speech or sermon. They are used to deliver a special kind of religious message, which sets King's statement apart from everyday speech. Some of the words he uses, such as *Hebrews, Israel,* and *Babylon*, relate to passages in the Bible. 2. Babylon was a wealthy and splendid city in ancient times. It gained its wealth because its king, Nebuchadnezzar, attacked Jerusalem. His armies captured the king, stole all the gold from the palace and temple, and exiled over 10,000 Israelites to Babylon. So the exiled Israelites saw the city as a place of imprisonment and slavery where they felt far away from God. 3. Though prosperous, Babylon was also a place of injustice and poverty. King argues that America is in danger of going in this same direction. He also wants to show how large, impressive cities and institutions are insignificant compared to God and his power. King uses Babylon to remind his congregation of their place in history.

Chapter Test   A. 1. d   2. d   3. c   4. b   5. c

B. 6. Nebuchadnezzar spent most of his reign in military campaigns to expand and maintain his empire. 7. Nebuchadnezzar used much of the wealth of the empire to rebuild its cities, especially Babylon. 8. Babylon would be overwhelming because of its size, the height of its buildings, and its varied population and languages.

C. Students' essays should include details about the Jewish revolt and the exile of the Jews to Babylon.

CHAPTER 23

Blackline Master

Nebuchadnezzar II: Years of Reign 605–562 BCE; *How became king* succeeded to throne; *Best known for* conquering other nations; *Building projects undertaken* restoring Babylonians cities, Processional Way, Ishtar Gate; *Babylonians' opinion of his rule* liked him, because he took part in New Year's Festival in Babylon; *How rule ended* died *Nabonidus: Years of Reign* 555–539 BCE; *How became king* after Nebuchadenezzar's death, three kings ruled in less than six years, and Nabonidus may have murdered the third one; *Best known for* not visiting Babylon for 10 years; *Building projects undertaken* rebuilding Sin's temple at Harran; *Babylonians' opinion of his rule* they did not like him because he didn't take part in the New Year's Festival in their city; *How rule ended* Nabonidus was defeated by Cyrus of Persia and lived in exile.

Chapter Test

A. 1. a   2. b   3. c   4. a   5. d

B. 6. Mesopotamian's believed that a visit from a god in one's dreams meant the god was sending a message to the person. 7. The New Year festival was important to Babylonians because they felt the prosperity of the city in the coming year depended upon the ritual. 8. Cyrus said that Marduk was unhappy with Nabonidus, and that he would return Marduk to his rightful place as king of the gods.

C. Students' essays should discuss how people who are unhappy with one ruler (Nabonidus) might be more willing to accept a different ruler (Cyrus).

THE ANCIENT NEAR EASTERN WORLD   **161**

CHAPTER 24/EPILOGUE

Blackline Master

Religion monotheism, Golden Rule; *Technology* wheel, plow, boat, irrigation canal; *Government* organization of cities and empires; *Law* first law collection, laws to prevent corruption, promote fairness, and foster justice

Chapter Test

A. 1. a 2. c 3. b 4. c 5. b

B. 6. Cyrus's kingdom of Persia was located in what is now Iran, on a high plateau in the Zagros Mountains. 7. Darius had an inscription carved on a mountainside at Bisitun to celebrate the glories of his reign. 8. Someone who cared for his family and obeyed the laws could expect to be rewarded with long life and good luck.

C. Students' essays should discuss one of the ancient Near Eastern concepts or innovations and how it is reflected in modern society.

WRAP-UP TEST

1. Students' essays should include farming near rivers to take advantage of floods, irrigation techniques, growing population, use of canals to irrigate more fields, and the invention of the plow.

2. Important components of civilization that developed during the Uruk period include cities with governments, organized religious practices, specialized workers, long-distance trade, classes within society, and a system of writing.

3. Students' steps should include clay tokens, tokens sent as messages in clay envelopes, pictures for tokens drawn on clay tablets, pictures of all sorts of nouns, pictures for other parts of speech, pictures that represented the sound of spoken words, pictures becoming more like designs, designs representing syllables.

4. Students' essays should include details from *The Epic of Gilgamesh* and discuss the characteristics and maturation of Gilgamesh that the Mesopotamians would have learned.

5. *How it was made known to the Babylonians* carved on a stone monument; *What kinds of cases it covered* divorce, arguments over property, duties to the king, criminal acts; *What kinds of punishments it handed out* fines, the criminal sometimes suffering the same fate as the victim; *What it said about the court system* the court system is powerful and everybody had better respect it.

6. Mesopotamian contracts were written for all sorts of transactions marriages, sales of goods and property, and so on. Students should describe the process of writing the contract and having witnesses sign the contract.

7. Advantages include solidifying alliances between kingdoms. Disadvantages include princesses being sent to faraway, alien lands and sometimes facing obstacles such as other jealous wives or disrespectful husbands.

8. Students' essays should explain that the Israelites had a strong feeling of being a nation separate from other peoples because of their history and their belief in a single god. This helped them keep their identity although they suffered exile and rule be different conquerors.

9. Students' Venn diagrams should show the differences and similarities of the Assyrians and Persians. Students should consider the empires' size, form of government, gods, ways of expansion, and ways of controlling the empire.

10. Students' essays should explain that after Alexander the Great conquered Persia, he made Greek the official language of Mesopotamia. Over the years, the people forgot Akkadian and Sumerian, could no longer read the old scripts, and began to forget the old stories. This was how the ancient Mesopotamian world disappeared.

ANSWERS FOR THE STUDENT STUDY GUIDE

CHAPTER 1

Word Bank/Word Play   Have students read sentences aloud.

Drawing Conclusions   1. a, c, d; 2. a, c, d; 3. b, c, d; 4. a, b, d.

Primary Sources   1. b, 2. d, 3. b.

CHAPTER 2

Word Bank   1. irrigated, 2. domesticated

What Happened When?

About 5000 BCE settlers established town on Eridu

Between 5000 BCE and 3000 BCE 18 shrines and temples built in Eridu

Sequence of Events   3, 8, 4, 6, 1, 7, 2, 5

Primary Sources   1. Ea, 2. fresh water, 3. more powerful than Ea, 4. *At your rising; the gods of the land assemble; Your fierce glare covers the land.*

CHAPTER 3

Word Bank   1. potter's wheel; 2. colonists; 3. millennium

Word Play   Check students' sentences.

What Happened When?

5000 BCE Southern Mesopotamia settled

3800 BCE Uruk period begins

3500 BCE pottery wheel, plow invented

3100 BCE Wheel and first wagon invented

Do the Math   4

Drawing Conclusions   1. b, c, d; 2. a, b, d; 3. a, b, d; 4. a, b, d.

Primary Sources   1. c, 2. b.

CHAPTER 4

What Happened When?

About 8000 BCE tokens first used

About 3350 BCE accounting tokens enclosed in clay balls

About 3200 BCE pictographic writing invented

About 3000 BCE cuneiform writing begins

About 2600 BCE first-known royal inscriptions

About 2400 BCE first personal letters written

Sequence of Events   1. before, 2. after, 3. after, 4. after, 5. before, 6. after, 7. before, 8. after.

Primary Sources   1. d, 2. c, 3. a, 4. b

CHAPTER 5

Cast of Characters

Shamash, also called Utu, was god of the sun

Ellil, also called Enlil, was leader of the gods.

Sin, also called Nana, was god of the moon

Anu, also called An, was god of the sky

Adad, also called Ishkur, was god of wind, storm, and war

Ishtar also called Inanna, was god of love and war.

Ea, also called Enki, was god of water

Mami was midwife of the gods

Ashur was god of the city of Ashur

Marduk was god of the city of Babylon

Check students' sentences.

Word Bank

1. d, 2. c, 3. d, 4. c

Main Idea   1. c, 2. d 3. b.

Primary Sources   1.c, 2. complaining, denouncing, muttering; 3. b

In Your Own Words   Have students read entries aloud.

CHAPTER 6

Cast of Characters

Sir Leonard Woolley: archeologist who discovered ruins of Ur
Queen Puabi: queen of Ur
Mebaragesi: king of Kish
Eannatum: ruler of Lagash

Word Bank   1. *nin*, 2. *lugal*, 3. *en*

Fact or Opinion?   1. opinion, 2. fact, 3.fact, 4. fact, 5. opinion, 6. fact, 7. fact, 8. fact.

Primary Sources   1. Eannatum and Urlumma; 2 Urlumma, 3. proud or arrogant, 4. Entemena

CHAPTER 7

Cast of Characters

Gilgamesh: ruler of Uruk
Enkidu: best friend of Gilgamesh
Sin-leqe-unnini: Babylonian poet, wrote *Epic of Gilgamesh*
Ut-napishtim: builder of boat in *Epic of Gilgamesh*

Cause and Effect   1. f, 2. b, 3. a, 4. e, 5. c, 6. d, 7. g, 8. i

Primary Sources   1. c

Do the Math   14 feet 8 inches tall

CHAPTER 8

Cast of Characters

Sargon: King of Akkad
Tira-il: scribe
Ibubu: palace steward
1. Mesopotamians 2. They had black hair

Word Bank   1. diplomat, 2. empire, 3. equid.

What Happened When?

2340 BCE Sargon came to power
Do the Math   2286 BCE

Drawing Conclusions   1. b, c, d; 2. a, b, d; 3. a, c, d; 4. c

All Over the Map   1.–3., 5. Check students' work against map on page 61; 4. Mediterranean Sea, Persian Gulf; 6. all distances are approximate: a. 600 miles, b. 1,100 miles, c. 1,500 miles, d. 600 miles; e. 600 miles; 7. Lumber and metals could now come from Sargon's empire once he conquered those lands so he would not need to import these materials from farther away.

CHAPTER 9

Cast of Characters

Enheduanna: daughter of Sargon

Word Bank   1. Nanna; 2. Ashimbabbar, 3. Inanna, 4. Ur.

Fact or Opinion?   1. fact, 2. fact, 3. opinion, 4. opinion, 5. fact, 6. fact, 7. opinion, 8. fact.

Primary Sources   1. radiant priestess, 2. b, 3. c, 4. b, c

CHAPTER 10

Cast of Characters

Shulgi: ruler of Ur
Hammurabi: ruler of Babylonia
Ur-Nammu: father of Shulgi
What Happened When?

2094 BCE Shulgi comes to power
1792–1750 BCE Hammurabi of Babylon reigns

Do the Math   2046 BCE

Compare and Contrast   Shulgi: 2, 3, 6, 7, 8, 9, 11; Hammurabi: 1, 4, 10, 12; Both: 5

All Over the Map   1. Check students' map against map on page 73; 2. about 425 miles; 3. about 175 miles; 4. a. east; b. north; c. northwest; d. north; e. Mari

CHAPTER 11

Cast of Characters

Ninshubur-tayar: Mesopotamian farmer
Patiya: workman, neighbor of Ninshibur-tayar
Samsu-iluna: son of Hammurabi
Shamash-nasir: adopted son of wealthy property owner

Main Idea   1. c, 2. a, 3. b, 4. c.

Primary Sources   1. robbery, 2. go to court 3. bring the merchant to court, 4. bring witnesses to identify property

CHAPTER 12

Word Bank   1. d, 2. b

Drawing Conclusions   1. a, b, d; 2. a, c, d; 3. a, b, d

Primary Sources   1. become a slave; 2. thrown out of house; 3. liberty

CHAPTER 13

Cast of Characters

Ur-Utu: wealthy man and priest in Sippar
Inanna-mansum: Ur-utu's father
Ilsha-hegalli: wife of Inanna-mansum
Ra'imtum: wife of Ur-Utu

Word Bank   c.

What Happened When?

1650 BCE Sippar destroyed
Do the Math   100 years

Sequence of Events   8, 1, 4, 3, 2, 7, 6, 5

Primary Sources   1. Rimum, 2. Bashtum 3. strangled, 4. pay alimony

CHAPTER 14

Cast of Characters

Pagirum: scribe who lived around 1650 BCE

1. wrote letters, 2. took dictation, 3. surveyed land

What Happened When?   2000 BCE Amorites invade Mesopotamia

Do the Math   Because the years from 100 BCE to 1 BCE make up the 1st century (compare 21st century CE)

Fact or Opinion?   1. fact, 2. opinion, 3. opinion, 4. fact, 5. opinion, 6. opinion, 7. fact, 8. opinion, 9. opinion, 10. fact.

CHAPTER 15

Cast of Characters

Shibtu: chief wife of Zimri-Lim
Zimri-Lim: king of Mari
Shimatum: daughter of Zimri Lim
Kirum: sister of Shimatum
Inib-sharri: daughter of Zimri Lim
Haya-Sumu: king, husband of Inib sharri

Point of View   1. S, 2. D, 3. D, 4. Z, 5. D, 6. D, 7. S 8. S.

All Over the Map   1. c, 2. a, 3. c, 4. d

CHAPTER 16

Cast of Characters

Samsu-ditana: king of Babylon
Mursili: king of Hatti
Hattusili: father of Mursili
Mursili

Word Bank   1. b, 2. d, 3. c

What Happened When?

1900 BCE Old Babylonian period begins
1792–1750 BCE Hammurabi creates Old Babylonian empire
1775–1761 BCE Zimri-lim of Mari, Syria reigns
1749–1712 BCE Samu-ilana of Babylon reigns

1650 BCE Foreign invaders destroy Sippar
1625–1595 BCE Samu-ditana of Babylon reigns
1595 BCE Old Babylonian Empire ends

Do the Math 1. 305 years 2. about 75 years younger

Sequence of Events 1. before, 2. before, 3. before, 4. before, 5. after, 6. after, 7. before, 8. after

All Over the Map Check students' work against map on page 104.

CHAPTER 17

Cast of Characters

Tadu-Heba: wife of Amenhotep
Amenhotep: ruler of Egypt
Tushratta: father of Tadu-Heba
Ammurapi: king of Ugarit
Tadu-Heba

Word Bank 1. a, 2. a, 3. d, 4. d. 5. b

What Happened When?

1595–1500 BCE Near East in turmoil
1500 BCE Kassites rule Babylonia, kingdom of Mittani begin; Hittite Empire grows
1387–1350 BCE height of international age
1185 BCE invaders destroy Canaan; Hittite Empire collapses
1176 BCE International Age ends

All Over the Map 1. Check students' maps against map on page 111; 2. all; 3. Egypt used the Nile; Babylon and Mittani used the Tigris and Euphrates; 4. Hatti controlled the city Ugarit, which was closest to the Mediterranean; 5. because it gave them access to trade with other cities and areas on the Mediterranean coast; 6. the city of Babylon, in the kingdom of Babylon

Drawing Conclusions 1, 2, 5, 7 10 checked

CHAPTER 18

Cast of Characters

Saul: king of the Israelites
David: second king of Israel
Samuel: religious leader
Ruth: Moabite woman
Naomi: mother-in-law of Ruth
Solomon: son of David
Omri: king of Israel
All are Israelites except Ruth.

Word Bank 1. c, 2. c, 3. b, 4. c; Hebrew; an author writes original material, A scribe copies information.

What Happened When?

About 1200 BCE Israelites came to the Levant.
1100–900 BCE dark age in Middle East
922 BCE Israel divides into two kingdoms

Do the Math About 1000 BCE

Main Idea 1.d, 2. a, 3. a.

All Over the Map 1.–2. Check students' maps against map on page 115; 3. about 75 miles; 4. west

CHAPTER 19

Cast of Characters

Noah, builder of an ark in Hebrew Bible
Abraham: original ancestor of Hebrew
Isaac: son of Abraham
Ishmael: son of Abraham
Jacob: son of Isaac
Joseph: son of Jacob

Compare and Contrast Israelites: 2, 3, 6, 7, 9 Mesopotamians: 4, 10. Both: 1, 5, 8

Primary Sources 1. Tigris, Euphrates; 2. freely of all trees; 3. eat from tree of knowledge; 4. Adam's rib

CHAPTER 20

Cast of Characters

Josiah: king of Israel
Moses: man who led the Hebrews out of Egypt

What Happened When?

About 1200 BCE Israelites arrive in Levant
About 1020 BCE Saul's reign begins
About 1000 BCE David's reign begins
About 960 BCE Solomon's reign begins
922 BCE Israel divides into two kingdoms
722 BCE Assyrian conquest of Israel
639–609 BCE Josiah rules Israel
598–597 BCE Jehoiakan of Judah reigns
587 BCE Babylonian exile begins
539 BCE Jews allowed to return to Jerusalem
After. The events take place in Israel, and Israelites first entered Israel after 1200 BCE

Cause and Effect 1. e, 2. d, 3. h, 4. b, 5. a, 6. g, 7. f

Primary Sources 1. b, 2. b, 3. a, 4. b, 5. Passover

CHAPTER 21

Cast of Characters

Ashurnasirpal: king of Assyria
Ashurbanipal: Assyrian king who had the first library
Sennacherib: king of Assyria
King Jehu: king of Israel
Ashurnasirpal conquered Jehu.

What Happened When?

9th century BCE Assyrian kings pushed beyond their borders
842–815 BCE King Jehu ruled
722 BCE Assyrians crushed Israel
704–681 BCE Sennacharib ruled Assyria

All Over the Map 1.–4. Check students' work against map on page 135, 5. about 950 miles wide and 1,050 miles long, 6. southwest, 7. Red Sea, 8. 400 miles, 9. Tigris, 10. Israel

Primary Sources 1. earth ramps and battering rams, 2. gold and silver, 3. They took all the funds from the temple, 4. He lost 185,000 men, 5. He did not want to admit his lack of power

CHAPTER 22

Cast of Characters

Nebuchadnezzar II: ruler of Neo-Babylonian empire
Jehoiachin: king of Judah
Nebuchadnezzar drove Jehoiachin from the throne.

Word Bank

1. Neo-Babylonian, 2. ziggurat, 3. kid gloves

What Happened When?
883–859 BCE Ashurnasirpal II reigns
704–681 BCE Sennacharib of Assyria reigns
649–547 BCE Adad-guppi, mother of Nabbonidus, lives
612 BCE Neo-Babylonian Empire begins
605–562 BCE Nebuchadnezzar reigns
555–539 BCE Nabonidus reigns

Fact or Opinion? 1. fact, 2. opinion, 3. fact, 4. opinion, 5. opinion, 6. opinion, 7. opinion, 8. fact, 9. fact, 10. opinion,

CHAPTER 23

Cast of Characters

Adad-Guppi: priestess, mother of Nabonidus
Nabonidus: ruler of Neo-Babylonian Empire
Cyrus: king of Persia
Cyrus conquered Babylon, which was ruled by Nabonidus.

Word Bank 1. b, 2. d.

What Happened When?

612 BCE Neo-Babylonian Empire beginning
610 BCE Harran is conquered
555 BCE Nabonidus becomes ruler of Neo-Babylonian Empire
542 BCE Nabonidus returns to Babylon
539 BCE Cyrus conquers Babylon

Primary Sources   1. C, 2. A, 3. A, 4. N, 5. N, 6. T, 7. T, 8. A

All Over the Map   1.–2. Check students' work against map on page 148, 3. a. 450 miles, b. 400 miles, 3. 400 miles, 4. Babylon, 5. c, 6. a

CHAPTER 24

Cast of Characters

Croesus: king of Lydia
Alexander the Great: Greek ruler
Darius I: king of Persia
Zoroaster: Persian teacher, founder of Zoroastrianism

Xerxes: son of Darius
Herodotus: Greek historian

What Happened When?

560–547 BCE reign of Croesus of Lydia
559–530 BCE reign of Cyrus of Persia
550 BCE Persian Empire founded
547 BCE Cyrus defeats Lydia
539 BCE Cyrus defeats Neo-Babylonian Empire
522–486 BCE Darius I of Persia reigns
490 BCE Persia attacks Greece
486–465 BCE Xerxes of Persia reigns
330 BCE Alexander the Great defeats Persian Empire
220 years

Drawing Conclusions   1. b, c, d; 2. b, c; 3. b, d; 4. a, b

All Over the Map   1.–3. Check students' work. 4. Caspian Sea, Black Sea; 5. Indus; 6. Jerusalem; 7. Lydia, Anatolia; 8. Israel, Judah

CPSIA information can be obtained
at www.ICGtesting.com
Printed in the USA
BVHW022136090123
655921BV00011B/295